T0114658

HeARTful Transformations
With The
ART OF TAPPING

The Only Self-Healing Guide You'll Ever Need To
HeARTfully Transform Trauma into Triumph

MONIKA MARGUERITE LUX

BALBOA.PRESS
A DIVISION OF HAY HOUSE

Balboa Press books may be ordered through booksellers or by contacting:

Balboa Press
A Division of Hay House
1663 Liberty Drive
Bloomington, IN 47403
www.balboapress.com
844-682-1282

Because of the dynamic nature of the Internet, any web addresses or links contained in this book may have changed since publication and may no longer be valid. The views expressed in this work are solely those of the author and do not necessarily reflect the views of the publisher, and the publisher hereby disclaims any responsibility for them.

The author of this book does not dispense medical advice or prescribe the use of any technique as a form of treatment for physical, emotional, or medical problems without the advice of a physician, either directly or indirectly. The intent of the author is only to offer information of a general nature to help you in your quest for emotional and spiritual well-being. In the event you use any of the information in this book for yourself, which is your constitutional right, the author and the publisher assume no responsibility for your actions.

Any people depicted in stock imagery provided by Getty Images are models, and such images are being used for illustrative purposes only.
Certain stock imagery © Getty Images.

Print information available on the last page.

ISBN: 979-8-7652-2608-7 (sc)
ISBN: 979-8-7652-2609-4 (e)

Balboa Press rev. date: 03/28/2022

ABOUT THE BOOK

The ART Of Tapping - EFT (Emotional Freedom Technique) unites with Expressive Arts Therapy, NLP, and a comprehensive collection of other energy healing and emotional release techniques to heal anxiety, trauma, and depression in a most loving way.

Discover a gentle emotional release technique that is part of "The BalanCHIng® Method" and "HeARTful Transformation Therapy", a unique, therapeutic system of healing that has liberated innumerable people from their emotional burden, opening the doors to greater levels of wealth, freedom, health, joy and fulfilling relationships by simply accessing and releasing what is buried deep within. This transformational method, developed by Monika Marguerite Lux, will take you on a journey to freedom in easy and playful ways, guiding you to release your past and create the future you truly want and deserve.

For more information or to book your HeARTful Transformation please visit:

- **www.balanching.org**

Contact me:

- **balanching@hotmail.com**

I believe that everyone wants to live a healthy and fulfilled life with meaningful relationships.

Negative experiences such as trauma, stress, and abuse can take us away from ourselves and our desired lives. Doing the self-love and self-growth work to get back on track is the best gift we can give to ourselves, those we love, and the world.

Do you know who you truly are and how to become your best self?

Do you know how to build the self-esteem and resilience to stay there and reach even further?

I can support you to achieve all of this and more!

What if you already had all the resources, you need inside of you to live your dream life?

How do you feel when you consider this possibility?

Dare to dream big about what might change for you if this were true?

I would love to take you to the next steps of your healing journey to transform trauma into triumph.

My sessions are intuitively guided to match the state and needs of my clients and reach maximum IMPACT.

And if you are looking for a **FREE online resource** to pursue renewal, wellness, and belonging, my YouTube Channel provides soul-care opportunities to increase your self-awareness and engage in exercises to bring you renewal, wellness, and belonging in your life.

Please subscribe to www.youtube.com/c/balanching

Are you ready to start your journey of self-discovery?

Welcome to The Art Of Tapping!

With this book, you can take back control of your life!

Oscar Wilde once said "I don't want to be at the mercy of my emotions. I want to use them, to enjoy them, and to dominate them." Remember, you are not your emotions!

All the effort you put into releasing trapped emotions will give you a sunnier outlook on life and teach you that you have a choice to feel good or not.

The root of all suffering is **separation from and denial of our divine origins (called "soul loss")**. Trauma is the **energetic imprint** of this division, a split in consciousness arising from adverse and unintegrated experiences, resulting in a fundamental **disconnect from who we are as divine beings,** felt most deeply in our hearts.

Disconnected from our soul's essence, we experience a loss of innocence. The purity of our nature and the depth of our pain is covered by layers of **"who we think we must be" to survive the unbearable and shadowy landscapes of false appearances and pretense.** Innocence is not safe when its vulnerability leaves us prone to all sorts of harm.

To heal and become whole, we must **reclaim our childhood innocence and reconnect with our soul being,** and be filled with gratitude to recognize all the miracles that happen in our lives every day.

We can only live a meaningful and purposeful life when we can remember, reconnect and **become WHO we were always meant to be by birthright**!

Let's start this journey NOW!

This book invites you to paint, draw, play, and experiment. It also invites you to tap on everything that comes to mind during the art process, even if it might sound, look or feel a bit crazy to you. Try to see everything through the eyes of a child.

Have the courage to acknowledge your trauma, show compassion and forgiveness for yourself, release your past and move on stronger than ever!

That's when you **transform trauma into triumph**.

HOW TO WORK WITH THE BOOK

Chapter One is all about LEARNING EFT Tapping & The 9 Gamut Procedure
Exercise muscle testing, learn the Tapping sequence. Once memorized, each round of it can be performed in about 30 seconds. It will take some practice, of course, but after a few tries, the whole process becomes so familiar that you can do it in your sleep. Apply it to any issue you want. If you get mega-stressed out in public, tap the side of the hand, and try to hold at least the frontal ESR points.

Chapter Two is all about CHANGING Limiting Beliefs
Find your core limiting beliefs, discover exciting ways to change them successfully with NLP. Become aware of your self-criticism and self-sabotaging thoughts and tap them away with EFT

Chapter Three is all about TRANSFORMING Trauma Into Triumph, by exploring a compilation of different emotional release techniques
With child-like curiosity, go on a journey of exploration and experimentation to find your personal emotional release technique that will always be on hand when required. Feel free to combine techniques and procedures like I use to do. Be spontaneous and have fun.

Chapter Four is all about HEALING Trauma with Expressive Arts Therapy & EFT Tapping
Let your creativity run wild. Don't overthink but savor the process. Get to know yourself along the way. Enjoy the flow state you may enter while creating art, as it is just as valuable as the final product.

Bonus
Tapping Scripts for Forgiveness, Grief, Gratitude, and Abundance

DISCLAIMER AND NOTE TO READERS

The information provided within this book is for general informational purposes only. While the author tries to keep the information up-to-date and correct, there are no representations or warranties, express or implied, about the completeness, accuracy, reliability, suitability, or availability concerning the information, products, services, or related graphics contained in this book for any purpose. Any use of this information is at your own risk. The material in this book is for informational purposes only. As each individual situation is unique you should use proper discretion, in consultation with a healthcare practitioner, before undertaking the exercises and techniques described in this book.

The author expressly disclaims responsibility for any adverse effects that may result from the use or application of the book. The direction given in the book is merely a guideline for its use.

The content of this book is not intended to be a substitute for professional medical advice, diagnosis, or treatment. Always seek the advice of your physician or other qualified health providers with any questions you may have regarding a medical condition. Never disregard professional medical advice or delay in seeking it because of something you have read in this book.

The methods described within this eBook are the author's personal thoughts. They are not intended to be a definitive set of instructions for this project. You may discover there are other methods and materials to accomplish the same end result.

This book contains references and links to other Third-Party products and services. Some of these references have been included for the convenience of the readers and to make the book more complete. They should not be construed as endorsements from, or of any of these Third Parties or their products or services. These links and references may contain products and opinions expressed by their respective owners. The author does not assume liability or responsibility for any Third-Party material or opinions.

All trademarks and brands within this book are for clarifying purposes only and are owned by the owners themselves, not affiliated with this document.

CONTENTS

PREFACE

You may ask me how the idea to write this book "HeARTful Transformations With The Art Of Tapping" was born.

Well, it all started when I was working with a teenager suffering from high levels of anxiety and panic attacks.

When I looked at her sitting across the table from me, I suddenly remembered my first encounter with art therapy and how deeply it had touched me as a client. Intuitively I felt that this was the only way to be able to build rapport and establish a safe place quickly.

I asked my client if she could draw on a piece of paper what happened when she was in a situation that induced a panic attack. She drew a picture with numerous shapes in different colors. Her hands were sweating, and I immediately started the tapping process.

"Even though I'm surrounded by so many different shapes, and it feels overwhelming and scary at times, I deeply and completely love, accept and forgive myself." We tapped on many aspects like "shapes moving around, while I feel paralyzed", "all the people looking at me and "I just don't know what to do… I'm so scared, I want to hide". After a couple of rounds, I saw the tension dissipate. My client opened her fists and her body started to loosen up more and more.

I asked her which of the shapes belonged to her and she told me that it was missing completely. We found out that her unique shape was the heart. "Wow," I said "that's the most important shape ever. It cannot be left out. Please add it to the other shapes." She drew a tiny heart because there was not much space left between the other shapes. I started tapping again "Even though I feel very small and unimportant, I deeply and completely love, accept and forgive myself." and "this tiny heart amidst all the big shapes… they are invading my space… they are intimidating… I don't feel safe…" etc.

"I would like to see a bigger heart." I encouraged her and she said, "There's no space; it would overlap the others." "That's ok," I answered and smiled at her. Now, she drew her heart in the middle of the picture, and indeed it was overlapping a few of the other shapes. We started tapping again: "Even though my shape is overlapping other shapes, I deeply and completely love, accept and forgive myself." "It is ok to overlap… it is ok to move as well… it is ok to interact… it can be fun to move and socialize with others… it might not be so difficult… it makes me curious to learn more about the others… what if it's exciting to mingle with different shapes…" etc.

We talked about how we can learn from others and how they can learn from us and a few sessions down the line she told me that her whole world and perspective had changed through exercises like that.

Now we were able to rewire the neurological pathways of the brain by applying new strategies for future scary moments and learning how to…

- recognize anxiety triggers quickly
- prevent panic attacks in their onset,
- use mindfulness exercises like breathwork, just tapping on the side of the hand or holding ESR points,
- reframing scary thoughts about the situation

Those steps helped build self-awareness and self-confidence. My client learned who she was at soul level and she became aware of her strengths and skill set. She discovered how fear and self-doubt robbed her of her full potential and how feeding her heart with self-compassion and self-forgiveness set her free and gave her wings to soar.

"As soon as you trust yourself, you will know how to live." — Johann Wolfgang von Goethe

"If you want to soar in life, you must first learn to F.L.Y (First Love Yourself)" – Mark Sterling

The transformational process was incredible. A shy teenage girl with anxiety and phobia turned into a social butterfly. Soon I got invited to a high school musical and with tears of joy filling my eyes I witnessed her performance as a dancer and singer.

And so I continued to focus on this new path that had opened before me. And finally, I decided that this technique had to be perpetuated in a book. Meanwhile, other energy healing techniques joined forces and this second edition will be a bit more comprehensive.

Testimonial:

After participating in conventional therapies, my teenage daughter who has crippling anxiety was more anxious than ever and began having panic attacks while out in public spaces, she was not able to go out unsupervised. We decided that she needed to try something different and found that Monika offered dance therapy which she was very excited about. After a few visits of Monika's unconditional support, kindness, acceptance, and love she began to trust and has excelled far beyond what we thought possible. She is now able to go out socially and has decided to go into public high school after being homeschooled for her whole life. Monika has helped to give her insight and control over her anxiety, and we thank her for changing our daughters' life!

Catherine C. and John B., British Columbia

QUOTES ABOUT TAPPING

I've always admired Louise Hay and read all her books. "Du kannst es! Durch Gedankenkraft die Illusion der Begrenztheit uberwinden" / "I can do it! How to Use Affirmations to Change Your Life" was my first book to buy while I have been studying Applied Kinesiology.

This is what Louise Hay says about EFT:

"Have you tried tapping yet? I've done a little bit of tapping in the past few months. I'm what you would call a "newbie" to the tapping world.

When I first heard about using tapping or EFT (Emotional Freedom Technique), I thought it was delightful that something this simple and easy could work.

Tapping, just like affirmations, is another wonderful tool that can help us to let go of our limiting thoughts and negative programming from our past.

And I do love the way the tapping process first releases the negative programming and then the affirmations help create more positive change and health in our lives.

Let's affirm: *Today I give myself the gift of freedom from the past. I tap with joy into the now.*"
https://www.healyourlife.com/have-you-tried-tapping

And here is another quote by Jack Canfield, originator of the #1 New York Times bestselling "Chicken Soup For The Soul" series and "Tapping Into Ultimate Success":

"EFT is the most powerful new transformational technology to come along in years..." https://www.healyourlife.com/tap-away-your-stress

CHAPTER ONE

PREPARATION

EFT TAPPING MANUAL

THE HISTORY OF TAPPING –
FROM TFT TO CLINICAL EFT

TFT – Thought Field Therapy

- Developer: Dr. Roger Callahan
- Developed From Ancient Meridian Energy Body Maps

Dr. Roger Callahan was the founder of tapping techniques and the person who discovered that by tapping on meridian points on the body, people started to feel better.

The story goes that his first TFT patient "Mary" had an intense water phobia. After 18 months of conventional therapy with Callahan, she would only reluctantly go near the edge of a swimming pool but no further, stating she had "awful feelings in her stomach."

Callahan then had the brain wave to ask Mary to think of the fear whilst tapping under her eye, which according to ancient energy body maps is linked to the stomach.

Without any other treatment, Mary suddenly exclaimed "It's gone! My fear of water, it's gone! I don't have those awful feelings in my stomach anymore!"

Over 30 years later, Mary is said to remain completely free of her phobia.

Callahan began experimenting with tapping meridian points and soon discovered that by bringing in other meridian points to tap on he could increase his success rate from an alleged 20% to 97%. His ideas were initially known as "Callahan Techniques" but later became Thought Field Therapy.

EFT - Emotional Freedom Techniques

- Developer: Gary Craig
- Developed From TFT, NLP

Born April 13, 1940, in the US, Gary Craig is a Stanford Engineer, Ordained Minister, and NLP Master Practitioner.

In 1991, Gary Craig became a student of Dr. Roger Callahan, founder of TFT, and over the next few years, he began to devise EFT as a "one-stop protocol" that would cover a multitude of problems by the concept of total redundancy.

"Rather than matching a problem to a tapping sequence, with EFT we only use one sequence and tap all the points for every problem. This is easier to learn and also takes the intuition out of the treatment flow making results more reliable to replicate." ~ Gary Craig

Another major difference between the two techniques is that TFT uses "muscle testing" as part of the treatment flow for gauging unconscious resistance, however, Gary Craig decided to remove this as it is "loaded for potential inaccuracy", especially in the hands of beginners.

Over the years EFT evolved to:

Positive/Energy/Optimal/Faster EFT, **Matrix Re-imprinting (Karl Dawson), Tapping Solution (Nick Ortner), Conscious EFT (NeftTi)**, etc.

THE IMPORTANCE OF RELEASING EMOTIONAL BAGGAGE OR 95% UNCONSCIOUS VS 5% CONSCIOUS

Neuroscience found that whenever there is a conflict between reason and emotion, human beings will always side with emotion. Why? Because emotion is the language of the subconscious mind. And we are constantly controlled by emotional survival patterns and beliefs we absorbed like sponges, especially during the first 6 years of our childhood. If we want to live a fulfilled, happy and healthy life we have to be aware of our present emotions and release the suppressed emotions of the past.

Often, we wonder why we reacted a certain way though we know better. Whatever worked as a survival pattern for us as children is still running as a subconscious program. But now it's time to replace it with a mature strategy.

Through emotional release, we can heal most aspects of our life, physical, mental, emotional, and spiritual.

When we get rid of our emotional baggage, we clear the way to manifest our true and highest potential.

CONTROL YOUR EMOTIONS - CONTROL YOUR REALITY

WATCH YOUR EMOTIONS BECAUSE THEY BECOME YOUR THOUGHTS

WATCH YOUR THOUGHTS BECAUSE THEY BECOME YOUR WORDS

WATCH YOUR WORDS BECAUSE THEY BECOME YOUR ACTIONS

WATCH YOUR ACTIONS BECAUSE THEY BECOME YOUR HABITS

WATCH YOUR HABITS BECAUSE THEY BECOME YOUR CHARACTER

WATCH YOUR CHARACTER BECAUSE IT BECOMES YOUR DESTINY

~ UNKNOWN

SELF MUSCLE TESTING - THE SWAY TEST

Muscle testing has proven to be an exceptionally helpful tool in the assessment of emotional imbalances and the evaluation of therapeutic options (trauma release).

It can help the practitioner to determine an individualized program tailored to the needs of a person:

- psycho-emotional issues like "What's the limiting belief that's keeping me stuck?",
- pain management like "Is the root cause of my chronic pain psycho-emotional?",
- diet management like "Are Gluten proteins causing my digestive problems?"
- allergy management like "Does my allergy has psycho-emotional roots?" or "Is this food causing the allergic reaction?"

The real challenges with muscle testing are the ability to step out of the equation for accuracy and the ability to work within the subtle areas of "inner communication".
But all this will come with practice and experience.

Before you start:

Cook's Hookup will hook up the electromagnetic energy your body and brain run on, so it's flowing smoothly again, and you won't be overwhelmed by fuzzy thinking.

- Cross one ankle over the other.
- Cross the same arm over the other.
- Your palms face each other.
- Join the fingers together and bring the hands under and up to the chest.
- Place the tongue on the roof of the mouth while breathing deeply.
- Stay in this position for a couple of minutes, breathing deeply and slowly.
- Switch legs and hands.

Muscle Testing

- Stand straight with your knees unlocked and your feet pointing directly forward. Relax your body with your hands hanging down loosely at your sides.
- Now you are ready to perform an accuracy check: First, make a statement or hold a thought in your head you know to be true for your "YES" response. (Example: "Is my name... (your name)?")
- Then make a statement that can only be answered with a clear "NO".
- Sense the response of your body for each answer — you should either feel yourself being gently pulled forward for a "yes" response or repelled back signaling it's not true or your body is not in resonance with that, which would be a "no" response.
- Now, you can test if you need to know more about the issue on hand or if you can already release it through the tapping process. If your subconscious tells you, you need to know more, you can ask the following questions:

- **When did this issue start?** During conception? During birth? Between birth and 5? 5 and 10? Etc.
  Example: If you get the answer "between birth and 5", you can ask for the exact age: with 5? With 6? Etc.
- You may also ask **who was involved**: My father, my mother, a teacher, a schoolmate, a partner, etc. If something pops into your head, you may ask: **Is this the incident that has to be dealt with and released?**
- It may take some practice to be accurate and consistent. Just keep at it though and you'll find a whole new way to communicate with your body through muscle testing.
- With this technique, you can even test food sensitivities. Place the substance you are testing in one hand and close your fist over it. Hold your hands up to your heart center, close to your thymus gland.
- Ask: "Is this good for my body?"
- Become still, centered, close your eyes, take a deep breath, and let go of expectations. After a few seconds, you become aware of your body either being pulled forward or falling backward.
- Muscle Testing will be one way to work with the two chapters about Core Causes and Core Limiting Beliefs.
- Remember, there are no mistakes! Just stay curious and playful, experiment, and enjoy every step of your healing journey.

BASIC PROCEDURE

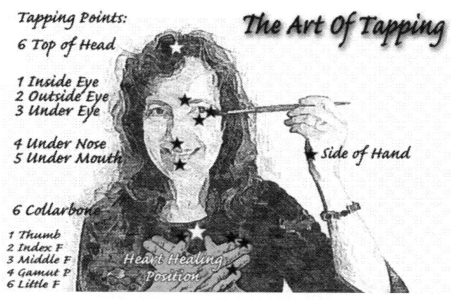

Tapping Points:

6 Top of Head

1 Inside Eye
2 Outside Eye
3 Under Eye

4 Under Nose
5 Under Mouth

6 Collarbone

1 Thumb
2 Index F
3 Middle F
4 Gamut P
6 Little F

The Art Of Tapping

Side of Hand

Heart Healing Position

Emotional Pain Scale

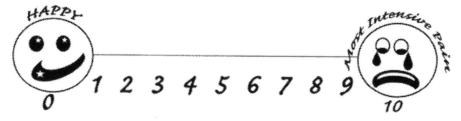

HAPPY

Most Intensive Pain

0   1 2 3 4 5 6 7 8 9   10

"Even though I'm feeling ... I deeply and completely accept, love and forgive myself"

"I choose to release the trauma and pattern behind the blocked emotion of ... that no longer serves me in a positive and productive way."

Even though I STILL have... Remaining

BASIC PROCEDURE

Step 1 Assume Heart Healing Posture (HHP) and take three deep breaths, in and out.

Step 2 Say the set-up statement and tap the Side Of Hand Point SOH (Small Intestine) or rub the Sore Spots (neuro-lymphatic points) to identify and correct psychological reversal, which is the subconscious state of self-sabotage.

Psychological Reversal occurs when our subconscious mind believes we should keep our chronic pain, extra weight, or bad habit rather than change.

According to the Kinesiology Institute (John Maguire), it makes quite a difference if you tap on the side of the hand continuously speaking out loud all of the following intention statements:

"I deeply and completely accept myself, even ...

1. Global   "… with all my problems, limitations, and challenges."
2. Future   "… if I will continue to have this challenge."
3. Deserving   "… if I don't deserve to get over this challenge."
4. Wanting   "… if I want to keep this challenge."
5. Possible   "… if I can't get over this challenge."
6. Allowing   "… if I will not allow myself to get over this challenge.

"I deeply and completely accept myself, even if…

7. Safe for self   "… it isn't safe for me to get over this challenge."
8. Safe for others   "… it isn't safe for others for me to get over this challenge."
9. Benefit to self   "… getting over this challenge will not be good for me."
10. Benefit of others "… getting over this challenge will not be good for others."
11. Necessary   "… I will not do what is necessary to get over this challenge."
12. Unique blocks   "… I have a unique block to getting over this challenge."

Step 3 Take a deep breath in and out before moving on to the next treatment point.

Step 4 Then continue to:

1. **Inside Eye (IE):**   **Bladder – Fear/Feeling Trapped**
2. **Outside Eye (OE):**   **Gall Bladder – Depression/Resentment/Indecisiveness**
3. **Under Eye (UE):**   **Stomach – Worry/Betrayal/Distrust**
4. **Under Nose (UN):**   **Governing Vessel – Feeling Inferior/Disconnection**
5. **Under Mouth (UM):**   **Central Vessel – Shame/Embarrassment/Bitter Humiliation**

Under Mouth and Nose can be tapped together and I call them "Nose & Chin" (N&C or vice versa)

Step 5   **Additional Points:**

Under Arm UA (Spleen – Lack of Control/Obsessive Thoughts/Hopelessness)
Rib point RP or LP under the breast (Liver – Anger/Aggressiveness/Envy/Vengeance)

Step 6   **Tap on Top Of Head TOH (Governing Vessel: anchoring/central nervous system) and Under Collarbone UC or CB (Kidneys – Death Fear/Terror/Dread) at the same time + switch hands (Head & Heart = HH)**

Step 7   **Assume the HHP (Heart Healing Position) for a moment of silent reflection. Take six deep breaths, in and out.**

Step 8   **Check your pain level on a scale from 0-10. (Subjective Units of Distress – SUD Level)**

Step 9   **SUD went down to 1 or 0   → CONGRATULATIONS**

Step 10   **SUD still above 1   → Next round: REMAINING "emotion/thought" PLUS 9 Gamut Procedure**

THE 9 GAMUT PROCEDURE

has a very useful function. ***It integrates both sides of the brain.*** It only takes about a minute to perform, and you can use it in the middle of a tapping sequence to increase the effectiveness of EFT or ***to get you 'unstuck' if you are not making progress.***

Start with a round of tapping in the usual way.

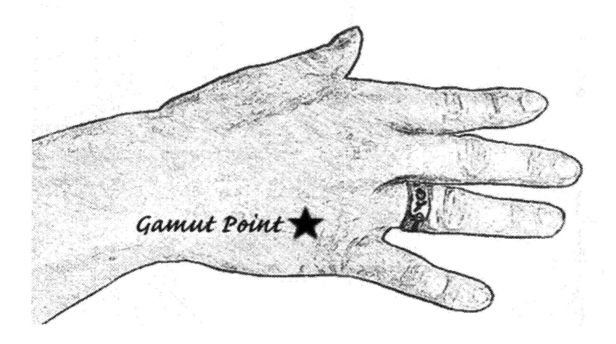

Gamut Point ★

Finger points can be added to your tapping routine, especially when you encounter stubborn issues. They are located at the side of the base of the nail.

1. **Thumb T (Lungs – Grief/Sadness/Cravings/Addictions)**
2. **Index Finger IF (Large Intestine – Rigidness/Defensiveness/Stubbornness)**
3. **Middle Finger MF (Circulation Sex/Heart Protector – Rejection/Abandonment)**
4. **Little Finger LF (Heart – Shock/Guilt/Lack of Emotion/Holding on to Hurt & Pain)**
5. **Gamut* GP (Triple Warmer – Confused Thinking/Instability)**

Then locate the Gamut point on the top of the hand, about an inch below the web between the small finger and the ring finger. Gently keep tapping on this point while focusing on the issue and doing the following:

- **CLOSE YOUR EYES then OPEN YOUR EYES**
- **Without moving your head… LOOK HARD DOWN TO YOUR RIGHT then LOOK HARD DOWN TO YOUR LEFT**
- **MOVE YOUR EYES IN A CLOCKWISE CIRCLE & AN ANTI-CLOCKWISE CIRCLE OR AN INFINITY EIGHT**

(HUM A FEW SECONDS of any song - COUNT OUT LOUD (1-2-3-4-5) - HUM a few seconds again (according to new scientific research this part can be left out))

*The Gamut point is also called "Brain Balancer" and it's *the one to tap for Hormonal Imbalance or symptoms like Hot Flashes*

AFFIRMATION TAPPING FOR EACH MERIDIAN

Tap on the related meridian point and say the affirmation out loud. Take a deep breath after each sentence. Start with the side of the hand and end with the baby finger. You may as well hold the fingers (Jin Shin Jyutsu – Japanese Self-Help Technique) and say the affirmation.

	Affirmations	**Meridian**
SOH	I feel warm, nurtured, loved, and connected.	Small Intestine
IE	I am in harmony, at peace and fully alive.	Bladder
OE	I reach out with tolerance and release all judgment.	Gall bladder
UE	I trust my gut feelings and the mystery of life.	Stomach
N&C	I am deeply grounded and standing tall.	Governing
C&N	I am clear, centered, and safe.	Central
UA	I have faith and confidence in my future.	Spleen
RP	I am kind, loving, and forgiving to myself.	Liver
CB	I step forward with courage. I open my heart to love.	Kidneys
T	I breathe in humbleness and breathe out faith.	Lungs
IF	I am relaxed and generous. I support my heart & soul needs.	Circulation-Sex
MF	I surrender and let go of the cords attached to the past.	Large Intestine
GP	I honor my inner Warrior; I am ready to overcome any issue.	Triple Warmer
LF	I love myself for who I am; my heart is filled with forgiveness.	Heart

HHP: Take 6 healing breaths

You may muscle test to find out which meridian needs your attention most and look at its meaning. Intuitively draw a picture of the issue (example: governing vessel = feeling inferior). Do you remember an incident as a child when you felt inferior? Tap on whatever comes up when you look at the drawing. Release it by taking 6 deep breaths while holding your ESR points.

WHAT TO DO WHEN EFT DOESN'T WORK (GARY CRAIG)

When properly applied by an experienced practitioner, EFT (Meridian Tapping) has a very high success rate, usually over 90 percent. However, the initial success rate for newcomers usually starts around 50 percent. When EFT doesn't seem to be working, one or more of the following factors are usually involved:

- The Set-up was not performed completely enough (Psychological Reversal)
- You are trying to apply EFT to more than one thing at a time (jumping thoughts)
- The problem is being approached too generally/globally/not specific enough

The EFT Set-up Phrase has not been performed completely enough
The Set-up phrase together with tapping on the side of the hand corrects for Psychological Reversal (PR). When PR is present it blocks the whole process from working. So, if you aren't getting anywhere, try to tap the side of your hand harder and with more than just two fingers or rub the Sore Spot more vigorously while very *emphatically* saying the affirmation out loud.

A "secondary gain" (hidden benefit) / blocking belief is interfering
A secondary gain is present when there is a "hidden benefit" or "hidden loss" to having or retaining the original issue. Examples of secondary gain include, "this issue keeps me safe," "I don't have to risk failure," "I get to avoid doing certain things by having this issue," and so on. Once you identify the secondary gain, you can tap on that directly. You should then be able to clear the original issue or problem more easily.

You are trying to apply EFT to more than one thing at a time
It is very important to tune into only one problem at a time. You sometimes may accidentally try to apply EFT to more than one thing at a time without realizing it. This can happen when you are distracted and are thinking about something else while you are tapping on your problem. This can also happen when a second issue gets activated while attempting to address an original issue, even if you are not overtly aware of it.

Original memories need to be addressed first
Sometimes, when we try to apply EFT to feelings about a current upset, it works fine. When this is not the case, it usually means that today's "charge" is really due to earlier similar formative

experiences in our past. In that case, EFT usually works better and faster by applying it to those earlier experiences first. Then the current experience will either already have been cleared up or be amenable to clearing with tapping. You can look for early memories by asking yourself what the current situation reminds you of from your past.

When nothing works and you are overwhelmed, please get help!!!

See contact information in the front of the book or watch some of my FREE self-help videos on YouTube!

PROXY EFT FOR BABIES, CHILDREN, AND PETS

Surrogate Tapping is also called "Proxy Tapping" because of the substitution of another person for the recipient of the tapping.

Whenever someone cannot do EFT on themselves and cannot have the EFT tapping done by someone else to them, like babies separated in an incubator or the severely ill (comatose patients) that cannot withstand the tapping, a substitute can take their place.

DON'T Necessarily Tap ON Your Animal!!

When people first find out about EFT for **babies, little children, people with dementia, the physically weak, those who are handicapped, and pets**, they immediately think that it is literally about tapping on them. But it might be very upsetting for babies and animals alike when they are tapped on AND your child might not be at home when experiencing a traumatic event. So, you tap on yourself to make the changes happen. That's when surrogate tapping comes in very handy.

Surrogate EFT works because fundamentally we are all energetically connected and One in Spirit.

The surrogate simply sets the intention through spoken words or thought, **"this tapping is for _____"**, filling in the blank with the name of the one intended to receive the benefits of the tapping.

It is important to **tune in or sense the emotions or state of distress of the other person (see Self I-Dentity through Ho'oponopono)** that the EFT tapping is intended to relieve. For example, if a baby is crying in a public place, tune in to the cry and just tap. What would be the suffering like? Let the words or thoughts come to you, like "I'm scared of the noise, people... I'm angry because I'm so hungry... etc."

And there is a benefit for you as well, called "borrowing benefit" in EFT. It simply means you heal yourself because you might have had a similar experience in your childhood like the person you're tapping for.

How Does Surrogate/Proxy Tapping Work?

When you keep the focus of your attention on a specific aspect of that energy system (a problem, disease, behavior, state of mind, etc.) and you change YOUR system by tapping on the points, YOU ARE ALSO CHANGING THEIRS through the energetic connection (the phenomenon of morphic resonance).

This was originally discovered when a lady, who was extremely distraught sitting by the side of her premature baby's incubator, unable to touch and hold them tight, treated herself to lower her and the baby's stress that was created by this situation. The baby responded by breathing more easily and slower and during the next "tapping" visits developed a strong will to survive while connecting deeply to the mother through her loving energy.

Since then, thousands of people all over the world have been astonished to find that by tapping on themselves whilst holding another living being's issues in their mind, they can make changes without touching them or even being in the same room.

1. Focus Your Intention: Tuning In

Think about the animal or baby and what it is specifically you would like to release, soothe, or change.

2. Make A Statement Of Intent: The Set-Up

Find a phrase or a sentence that describes the problem succinctly and clearly to you. For pets, you could say for example, "Tom has this terrible allergy." or "Sam never stops barking." or, "This brown horse is distressed." if you don't know the animals' name.

3. Tap the EFT Round(s) as often as needed until you feel good and positive within.

Try it on EVERYTHING:

- training problems
- health problems
- relationship problems like jealousy, aggression
- attention-seeking behaviors, repetitive behavior disturbances
- stress and nervousness, fears, phobias, self-esteem, unhappiness, resentfulness, lack of social skills

- sadness, depression, lack of joy in life
- pain, discomfort, disturbance, disease, allergies, past traumas, mistreatment, mishandling, misuse

IMPORTANT!

The surrogate needs to "keep themselves out of the way" (quote Gary Craig). This means that the surrogate's attention and intention need to be **free of personal views, opinions, and the personal sense of "self" or EGO.** This allows the surrogate to serve as a **"clear channel"** without personal bias and interpretation of the situation.

In many cases, it is impossible to get verbal permission from the person being served. The surrogate tapping is offered with the intention of it being a gift, blessing, similar to offering a prayer. You can also ask for permission through muscle testing.

Prayer: *Thank you, Spirit, for your guidance and help in channeling healing energy for the highest good of …*

ESR – EMOTIONAL RELEASE POINTS

I have helped clients release even deep-seated emotional trauma (a mother who ran over her child with the car) with the Emotional Stress Release (ESR) technique. The Frontal Points are on the Frontal Eminences of the forehead, on the prominences above the eyes (Glabella) and the other two points are at the base of the skull on the occipital eminences. Lightly holding these two areas by placing one hand across the forehead and the other on the base of the skull can have a profound calming effect in any anxiety-provoking, overwhelming or stressful situation. This hold opens the mind to an adaptive rather than protective response to present, past, or anticipated stress or trauma.

Release Process Example

Work-Finances-Relationships-Family-Spiritual-Health → EXAMPLE

1.	What area would you like to work on?	Relationships
2.	What would you like to change?	My response to my husband's criticism
3.	How do you react now?	I immediately start yelling
4.	How do you want to react?	In a calm way
5.	What does his criticism mean to you?	I'm not good enough.
6.	Not good enough for what?	Not good enough to make as much money as him
7.	Why is that important for you?	My father said "Businesses are for men and men are providers. A woman's job is to raise children and be a mother."
8.	So, it's about a limiting belief that you adopted in your childhood?	I guess so.
9.	Let's tap on this limiting belief….	I replace the belief with "I am capable of having a successful business and earning my living."

10. Tapping protocol plus…
   - checking SUD
   - checking what else is needed, like eye movements, **ESR Points** or Breathing, etc.

You can also walk in figure eights, speaking the new belief out loud to MANIFEST it.

EFT STORIES

My own stories

I have been doing EFT Tapping for 17 years. I started by studying Applied Kinesiology. First, I learned how to test 42 muscles in Touch For Health. Then it was about 14 muscles and I thought "yep, slowly we are going to approach a technique that resonates with me." I learned about Roger Callahan and his approaches toward phobias, and finally, I was taught the EFT Tapping process that Gary Craig had developed. I immediately fell in love with this fast and effective technique that could be taken anywhere and used anytime. Meanwhile, it became second nature to me. When I wake up from a nightmare in the middle of the night, I tap myself back to sleep in my mind. Yes, that's right, I don't do the physical tapping because I'm too tired. I can internally feel myself tapping on all the points when I do it mentally and focus on the intention of going back to sleep as fast as possible.

"Our intentions create our reality. Intentions directly affect our metabolism and consequently every aspect of our health. It is common knowledge in the scientific community that our intentions influence our healing processes." ~ Dr. Adam McLeod

Of course, I use EFT during the day as well, as soon as I get triggered and feel emotionally out of balance.

1. Story: The Black Bag In The Middle Of The Street

I was on my way to work when my eyes caught a black plastic bag in the middle of the road. Tears were shooting into my eyes and my heart felt heavy, filled with all that devastating sadness. But I didn't have to dig deep to know what was going on at this very moment. I just knew. About 12 years ago, I was on my way to work when I saw something black lying in the middle of the road. First, I thought it could be dirt lost by a truck or a black garbage bag. As I came closer, I had to discover that my black and white cat had been killed by a car. I was inconsolable and desperate. It had been the third cat that was ripped out of my life and my heart broke in pieces. As a therapist, focused on emotional release I had worked on and through those deaths multiple times and everything seemed dealt with. But with time and studying EFT in-depth, I learned that an incident has many aspects.

Gary Craig refers to the term "aspects" as "parts" of an event. Within those events, aspects are the parts of the experience, and it's vital to identify all the aspects of an event and tap on each one till it loses its emotional charge.

Obviously, I had overseen an aspect of this past traumatic event, or I had not allowed myself to grieve properly and therefore had been triggered again by the plastic bag. I immediately started to tap the side of my hand against the steering wheel, saying the affirmation and then tapping through the sequence. I had released the aspect before I arrived at work and felt totally calm and balanced again.

2. Story: The Steep Hill

Another incident happened some years ago in Manitoba when I accompanied a farmer to an abandoned farm in the prairies. We had to take a gravel road and drive down a narrow and very steep hill to get to the property and I felt panic coming up inside of me. I started to shiver while my heart was racing, and I grabbed whatever I could to hold on. Of course, I was unable to explain why I was so scared going down that hill. For the entire ride, I was wondering about my extreme reaction and if it had to do with my fear of heights. At home, I tapped and tapped for hours but nothing seemed to come up, which is very unusual for me and my infallible intuition. I decided to let go of the "why" and see what would happen.

After three days, it popped up very suddenly while I was sitting in my car, driving to work. I remembered that I had tried to please my father and get his attention and love during my whole childhood. I knew that he loved skiing, so I wanted to learn this sportive activity to accompany him on his vacations, usually a couple of weeks during the winter when he left for Switzerland. He never even asked my mom and me whether we would like to come with him. My father was a very impatient man who didn't want to be bothered by children and their questions. He often yelled at me when I didn't understand what he meant on the first go. In this case, I had convinced him to teach me how to ski. He had shown me the snowplow technique in front of our home and the following weekend he took me to my first ski hill. I had never seen a ski lift before and started to get anxious, but he took me between his legs in front of him and we managed to arrive at the top of the hill. Up there he reminded me of the technique and encouraged me to go downhill. I looked down and it seemed too steep for me. I started to shiver, sweat, panic, and cry. My father got very angry and yelled "Do you think I wasted time and money for you to chicken out now? Do you think I have nothing better to do? Do you think I will ever again listen to you begging me to show you something and then be too dumb and too afraid to do it? Do you think your cousin would be such a coward? What did I do to deserve such a daughter?" and then he pushed me hard. Of course, I lost balance, fell, lost a ski, slid down the hill, and cried until we arrived at home, feeling more rejected, unworthy, and unloved than ever.

This had been the first and last time in terms of downhill skiing. I had never approached this sport again until I tried and enjoyed cross-country skiing after immigrating to Manitoba.

Anyways, I pulled my car to the side and tapped on the incident with all aspects that came to mind, and indeed, the next time we drove to the farm, I was only left with my fear of heights which is pretty manageable.

You may ask why I don't tap on my fear of heights. I know that the subconscious mind protects us all the time. My fear of heights protected me from jumping from a bridge when I was suicidal around my twenties. I'm very grateful to be alive and I guess, I still want to keep my lifesaver, even though it's sometimes a bit uncomfortable.

3. Stage Fright

I have been raised overprotected and pretty much imprisoned in our family home. Friends were "chosen" and if they were "not suited" in my mother's point of view removed again. Most of my childhood I spent alone, living in my fantasy world. I was scared of going out in public. I was fed up with being hurt. And it was horrible enough to be wounded by one's own parents; I didn't want to suffer anymore. It felt as if the scars would never be able to heal anyway. But finally, my soul found an escape route. Every time I suffered overwhelm, I got sick (chronic Gastritis) or I fainted.

That way I made it through school without ever having to speak in front of the class or other people. I had always admired my father for being able to hold speeches at his fraternity meetings, but later on, never thought about it anymore. Of course, at the time of immigrating to Manitoba, I was pretty self-confident after studying Applied Psychology, Kinesiology, NLP Coaching, and Systemic Family Constellation for almost 3 years.

I wasn't scared at all when I was left alone in a strange country because my husband had to return to Germany for two months just after we had decided where we wanted to move. I felt excited and adventurous, got all the licenses and cards while he was abroad, moved to the little hobby farm on my own, and made my first friends pretty quickly.

I also had my first job in a heartbeat and started as a barista for fancy coffee drinks and lattes in a rustic coffee shop. One day a lovely lady walked in and we started to chat while she was waiting for her Mocha. It turned out that she was the chairwoman of the Rotary Club and the manager of the Royal Bank of Canada.

She told me that the speaker for the next Rotary meeting had canceled and that she thought energy medicine could be a great topic for the members to learn about. "Would you like to be our next week's speaker?" she asked me and before she even had finished the question I almost yelled "yes", feeling so thrilled because somebody in my new home country showed interest in what has been my biggest passion for so many years, helping people heal through energy medicine and psychology.

After she had left it suddenly occurred to me that this would be my first presentation and speech on stage in front of people. My English wasn't as good as it is now and so I approached the literacy department of the career center which helped me get my job. Together with my teacher I wrote about 4 pages, almost like an essay. For the next two days, I read the script over and over again. One day before the presentation I ripped it into pieces and wrote it in my own words. On the way to the meeting, I got very nervous, and anxiety started to creep up inside of me. I parked my car, ran into the washroom, locked the door, and started tapping. After about 5 rounds I was so calm and confident as if I had done presentations all my life.

I stepped on stage, did my thing, and enthusiastically listened to the applause. I will never forget the moment when the nice chairwoman stood up, thanked me, and said "This was a banker's speech". And I stepped up from being a barista to a CSR position at RBC. Since then, I love doing presentations and sharing my story on how I was able to transform my childhood trauma into triumph and how I can help others to do the same.

"We are not defined by what happens to us, but by how we choose to respond." ~ Turia Pitt

4. The ESL Course

After moving to Vancouver Island, I decided to enroll in the "**English as a Second Language**" (ESL) Program at the university that prepares immigrant and international students to achieve their academic, vocational, and personal goals.

In one of the lessons, we had to watch a movie on how students with Dyslexia were misunderstood and treated unfairly by the teachers. I was tearing up as I started remembering when I was ridiculed by a Physics teacher in front of the class. I had not been able to explain an electric circuit and he grabbed my arm, pulled me to the front, and started to make fun of me, rubbing his plastic comb and holding it over my head to make my hair stand up. The classroom was screaming and laughing while I stood there paralyzed with fear and tears rolling down my cheeks. It felt to me as if the humiliation lasted forever.

As it would have been awkward to cry during the movie at ESL class, I started tapping on the side of the hand, taking deep breaths, and saying in my head "Although I had been ridiculed in front of the class and it felt devastating at that time, I deeply and completely love, accept and forgive myself." I imagined how I hugged my inner child. I told this little girl that I was here for her and that I would never let anything like this happen to her again. I calmed right down and stayed relaxed till the end of the movie.

"Caring for your inner child has a powerful and surprisingly quick result: Do it and the child heals." - Martha Beck

Of course, there are many more stories, but I think, these 4 can give you a pretty good picture of walking the talk or applying the techniques I teach.

The Sore Shoulder

In one of my seminars, I had a client with a sore shoulder. I explained to her that pain and disease are often caused by buried emotions and then asked her when it started. She told me about a car accident almost 20 years ago and that she'd got away just with some bruises. The doctors always had reassured her that everything had been fine with her shoulder. I encouraged her to tell me about the accident as I intuitively felt it was linked to the pain in her shoulder. At first, she refused, telling me that it had happened so long ago, that she had dealt with this incident already, and that she didn't want to talk about it again. But I could see how nervous she got and that her body started to shake. I took her hand and just tapped on the Gamut point and the side of her hand while she tried hard to fight back the tears forming in her eyes. I kept on tapping until she started to relax and stop crying.

Again I encouraged her to share her story about the accident and promised her that it would be very healing to tap through the whole traumatic experience. Her voice trembled when she gathered all her courage and revealed all the aspects of…

- being called by one of the 16-year-old clique members who had gotten a hold of dad's car, inviting my client for a ride to the lake
- convincing her best friend to accompany her although she did not agree to do something illegal
- the moments of the accident when they collided with another car and rolled over into the ditch
- her best friend being catapulted out of the car because of not being buckled up
- kneeling next to her best friend, thinking she was dead
- seeing the ambulance drive away with her best friend
- coming to the hospital and learning that her best friend would end up in a wheelchair, paralyzed for the rest of her life,
- visiting a couple of times but then being too scared to face reality and rather running away
- not being able to establish contact anymore about 10 years later, having lost sight of each other

With every emotional release, my client became calmer, and, in the end, she was at peace. She was able to move her arm freely and without pain. This proved again, that suppressed emotions can be the root of disease, pain, depression, and PTSD (Post Traumatic Stress Disorder), to name some examples.

The main aspect we discovered was of course the crippling emotion of GUILT. My client had convinced her best friend to join the "gang" on this trip and this young girl of all people was the most injured passenger. In fact, she became paralyzed through this accident. Can you imagine, how this burden may cause shoulder pain? Going through the trauma again was causing a lot of emotional pain and many tears were cried through the process. But in the end, my client was free; free of guilt, and free of pain.

Weight Loss

I once worked with a client who had tried to lose weight for almost ten years and it had been an up and down, losing and regaining all the time. My client was very frustrated and at the end of her wits as she had tried everything, from consulting nutritionists, trying all kinds of diets to visiting various doctors without any results.

I am very intuitive and when I work with somebody, I connect to the energy field very quickly. I sensed that this issue had its roots in her childhood. I decided to do a family constellation (Bert

Hellinger: "Orders Of Love", "Acknowledging What Is", "Movement Of The Soul"). Usually, this is a type of group therapy but it's possible to do it one-on-one, using objects, figurines, stuffed animals, Lenormand cards, or floor anchors to represent the family members or the issue. So, I let her choose representatives for herself, her siblings, and her parents and asked her to put them intuitively in the middle of the room.

I was surprised to see her and her siblings standing in a row one behind the other, facing the father and I asked her what she thought about this picture. She got very emotional and told me that once a week her father used to spank all the children with a belt for disobedience. The youngest sister had been obese and received the harshest punishment.

"How many of your siblings are overweight right now?" I asked her immediately and she told me that all of them had some weight issues.

I explained to her that there are invisible unconscious loyalties among family members and that taking on weight out of blind love, to protect the younger sibling was an attempt to bring balance back to the family system. Therefore, all the other siblings took on some weight. I invited my client into the constellation, to step into her place ("Knowing Field") and tell her sister "I did it for you to protect you and to take away some of your pain that weighed you down. I was the older one, I was able to carry more weight than you. But now we are all adults and it's not necessary anymore. Now I finally can let go of the weight and so, I choose to let go."

Then, we started tapping on every aspect of the trauma, releasing the hidden and destructive family dynamics of her childhood. We tapped on forgiveness for self and others, acknowledging that every family member has his or her very own story and destiny.

I told my client that the parents of our generation still had to deal with war trauma and shared my own family history:

"All her life, my mother had been depressed because of her traumatic war experience, fearing for her life during the many air raids when she was sitting in the bomb shelter, not knowing if she was able to return to her home or ruins. And my grandmother had to flee from the Red Army with my father and his brother in a cold and overfilled train, relocating from Breslau (Wroclaw, Poland) to Rosenheim (Germany). My grandfather had been missing in action and it took the White Cross ten years after the war to inform my grandmother about his death that had occurred in a Russian prison camp. She had been waiting for her husband for ten years because she didn't want to believe that he wasn't alive anymore, after all, she had a letter where he had promised to come back."

EFT Tapping and the insights from the constellation finally helped my client to lose weight for good without gaining it back.

The fairy and the bowl of porridge

Back in Germany, I had an appointment with a very good friend who is a hairdresser and at that time worked out of her home. I learned that her youngest daughter just had come down with the flu and was asked if I would mind her looking after her little one from time to time. Of course, I also wanted to see how Anna Lena was doing as I loved this little red-haired girl very much. Soon she was sitting on my lap, not able to sleep any longer. I felt how feverish she was and started to give her a Reiki treatment while I was holding her in my arms. My friend invited me to stay for lunch and had prepared a bowl of porridge for her daughter. But of course, there is a lack of appetite that comes with flus and colds, and I pondered how to convince her to at least eat a little bit.

The girl gave me a clue. She was looking all around the room to find her fairy but couldn't see her. I told her that I could see fairies too and that I had discovered this magical being sitting on the rim of the bowl. "Oh dear," I screamed out loud "it fell into the porridge." The child asked me how we could help the fairy quickly, and I said "Only you can save the fairy from drowning in the porridge. But it's an easy task. You just have to eat it. Then, the fairy will be able to touch the ground with her feet and climb out of the bowl."

Anna Lena ate all of her porridge. I told her that the fairy wanted to reward her with some healing magic and we started to tap while I quickly made up this rhyme:

> There is a secret language that only fairies know.
> It's about tapping some points in a row.
> It's about rubbing a place where you're sore.
> And a magic sentence with nine words or more.
> The fairy asks, "Does it feel better a little?"
> The child laughs "I feel as fit as a fiddle!"

I taught my friend the tapping sequence and her daughter was not only able to heal herself from her flu very quickly but to use this tool to get rid of any stressful stuff she brought home from school, as EFT Tapping can be used for bullying issues, fear of exams, and more.

TESTIMONIALS

It was curiosity that drove me to make my appointment with Monika M. Lux. It wasn't until after I had my first treatment from Monika that I found out the meaning of Energy Healing or Energy Therapy. During this first counseling session Monika asked a few, but pertinent, questions that led to rediscovering old wounds.

These old wounds manifested in phobias for certain situations which led me to flee, for many years, unbearable to me, but perfectly normal social situations. Monika proceeded with an Emotional Freedom Technique (EFT) or Tapping as it is also known.

At first, I wasn't sure what this was meant to do, but I followed her direction nevertheless, and shakily tapped along and repeated her words. After the tapping session was completed, Monika asked the question "How does it make you feel when you think of the social situation?" I thought and imagined but felt neither agitation nor fear.

It has been four years, and to this date, the phobia, which used to send me running for so many years of my life, has never resurfaced.

I am utterly and deeply grateful to Monika and her ability to skillfully apply her psychological counseling knowledge and integrate it with the various energy treatment modalities she utilizes in her praxis.

Grace S., Lake Audy, Manitoba

As I continued losing body mass from Chemo, physical weakness became a serious problem at times. This was only compounded by a complete loss of appetite. Working on my meridians with Applied Kinesiology and EFT went along with restoring proper re-aligned strength and the determination to eat at all costs.

I have had digestive problems all my life which certainly contributed greatly to my current cancer issues. It was only after THREE sessions of re-aligning and balancing meridians that my whole digestive tract calmed right down. No more bloating, reflux, diarrhea, etc. I was wondering "So, this is what it's like to feel "normal"? Wow!". I feel great and truly appreciate for the first time in my life having a HAPPY digestive system.

My physical body became more balanced, and my mind became more balanced too – no irrational or fearful thoughts or worries.

I have learned EFT (Emotional Freedom Technique) with Monika in a group workshop in 2008. The basic recipe with positive affirmations from the sessions helped me move away from negative thoughts. "Downtimes" are fewer and less exhaustive. Tapping helps remind me that I can control my thoughts and it's very affirming. EFT has very much helped me control anxiety and worry, especially in this past year of illness. And there's still a work in progress…

Jeff K., Erickson, Manitoba

Most workshops are inside a building with artificial light and in a big city. So, I appreciated it a lot to be able to sit outside for the whole day and enjoy the beauty of this unique place and the summer weather while learning about the Emotional Freedom Technique. The workshop was well organized and thanks to Monika's husband we had snacks in the morning, an awesome lunch, and coffee in the afternoon. Everything was explained in a well understandable way, even for people who had no idea about Meridians or Energy healing. Monika is a very humorous instructor and intuitively creates a lot of metaphors which really made this workshop a very unique and vivid experience. In the afternoon, we worked on our personal issues on a one-to-one basis while the others could watch and learn how to dig deeper and discover the important aspects. I first thought it would be boring just to watch, but the way Monika was counseling the workshop members was such an exciting experience I would not have wanted to miss. Thanks to Monika and her husband for that great day.

Ashley W., Val Marie, Saskatchewan 2008

CHAPTER TWO

CHANGING LIMITING
BELIEFS WORKBOOK

- The 6 "Lifetraps" Of Self-Limitation
- How To Approach Limiting Beliefs The NLP-Way (Uncover & Transform Limiting Beliefs On Your Own)
- NLP Ecology Check
- NLP Disney Strategy Constellation With Eye Cues
- NLP Magic Wand Exercise To Evaluate New Beliefs
- EFT Tapping For Fear Of Change
- Core Causes Work Sheet (Become Aware Of Negative Self-Talk & Self-Sabotage)

CORE LIMITING BELIEFS – THE SIX "LIFETRAPS" OF SELF-LIMITATION

What to do?

First, muscle test the category A, B, C, D, E, or F, for example, asking "Is my belief in category "A"? Then, test the list by speaking out loud the limiting belief statement, being aware of your body's reaction. After identifying the belief, let's say "I'm inferior", you could ask at what age it was formed. Sometimes beliefs are created

- during conception, if there was abuse involved,
- or during pregnancy when there was trauma or conflict
- or during birth, when there were difficulties (forceps, mother at risk, etc.)
- during your own life
- generational or ancestral
- from another lifetime

You could also ask who was involved, followed by "Do I need to know more?" or "Can I release this belief now?"

Now, that you know everything you need to know you can start tapping. Perhaps you even remember a certain situation when you felt inferior. Tap on everything that comes to mind.

Finally, replace the old belief with a new one, like "I am enough".

How does it feel? You can ask for the percentage of belief integration. If the new belief still cannot be integrated, ask if there's another layer to be released?

Even if you are "computer savvy", it might be quite exhausting to scan through all the folders and subfolders to uncover your subconscious programming. But with the help of self-muscle-testing, you can take a shortcut.

A) Defectiveness Beliefs

reflect a general sense that one is inherently flawed, incompetent, or inferior. Often, people who maintain thoughts characteristic of a defective core belief withdraw from close relationships in fear that others may discover that there's something wrong with them at the core. Examples of thoughts patterns characteristic of defectiveness include:

- I'm not good enough - I'm stupid – I'm a failure
- I can't get anything right - I do everything wrong
- I'm inferior - I'm worthless – I'm insignificant – I'm useless
- I can't measure up to others (comparison)
- I'm always number two - I always finish last
- I'm unattractive (ugly, fat, etc.)
- There's something wrong with me
- I don't deserve anything good
- I'm always wrong (generalization)

B) Unlovable beliefs

often cause people to make assumptions about the extent to which they belong and question whether they deserve love or can be loved. Individuals who believe they are unlovable may withdraw from relationships or maintain superficial companionships to avoid the suspected pain that will arise when they are inevitably rejected. Furthermore, the belief that one is unlovable can lead to significant feelings of loneliness even in the presence of others. Some thoughts related to an unlovable core belief include:

- I'm not lovable – I'm unacceptable – I'm unlikeable
- I'm always left out - I don't fit in anywhere
- I'm alone - I don't matter
- I'm not wanted - I'm not welcome – I don't belong
- Nobody loves me – Nobody wants me
- I'm bound to be rejected

C) Abandonment Beliefs

create assumptions in people that they will lose anyone to whom they form an emotional attachment. Abandonment and unlovable core beliefs can often be related or even the same. Often, those concerned with abandonment believe that people will ultimately leave, which will result in misery and loneliness. Consequently, people with abandonment beliefs almost constantly seek attention, reassurance, and silence opinions out of fear that others will desert them in the presence of differing viewpoints. Examples of thoughts related to abandonment can include:

- People I love will leave me
- I will be abandoned if I invest in loving or caring for something/someone
- I am uninteresting, and people will not see me because of it
- If I assert myself, people will turn away from me
- I can't be happy if I'm on my own/alone
- I'm bound to be rejected/abandoned/alone

D) Helplessness/Powerlessness Beliefs

Generally result in people assuming they lack control and cannot handle anything effectively or independently. Individuals who believe they are helpless often face difficulties making changes. Furthermore, a sense of powerlessness can cause people to become victims who try to over-control their environment. Some common thoughts reflecting helplessness/powerlessness core beliefs include:

- I'm helpless/powerless
- I'm out of control and I must have control to be okay
- I'm weak/vulnerable/needy
- I'm trapped and can't escape
- I'm unsuccessful - I can't achieve anything
- I can't change - There's no way out
- I can't handle anything - I'm ineffective
- Other people will manipulate me and control my life
- If I experience emotions, I will lose control
- I can't do it (right) - I'm a loser/failure
- I can't stand up for myself - I can't say "no"

E) Entitlement Beliefs

are sometimes not entirely apparent, but reflect a belief related to specialness that causes individuals to make demands or engage in behaviors regardless of the effect on others. Those who maintain an entitlement core belief assume they are superior and deserve a lot of attention or praise. Often, people develop an entitlement core belief to compensate for feeling defective or socially undesirable. This can lead to unreasonable demands that others meet your needs, rule-breaking, and resentment of successful others. Some entitlement-related beliefs include:

- If people don't respect me, I can't stand it
- I deserve a lot of attention and praise
- I'm superior/better than others (entitled to special treatment and privileges)
- If I don't excel, then I'm inferior, worthless, and just end up ordinary
- I am a very special person (and other people should treat me that way)
- I don't have to be bound by the rules that apply to other people
- If others don't respect me, they should be punished
- Other people should satisfy my needs
- People have no right to criticize me
- Other people don't deserve the good things that they get
- People should go out of their way for me
- People don't understand me - get what I mean (because I am special/brilliant/etc.)
- I can do no wrong - I'm always right

F) Caretaking/Responsibility/Self-Sacrifice Beliefs

could be separated into independent categories, but they reflect similar beliefs and can be addressed as a group. Self-sacrifice beliefs refer to the excessive forfeit of one's own needs in the service of others. Individuals often feel guilty and compensate by putting the needs of others ahead of their own. Such people often believe they are responsible for the happiness of others and apologize excessively. Responsible individuals may take pride in their diligence and dependability, without necessarily feeling a need to care for others or engage in self-sacrifice. People who maintain core beliefs rooted in caretaking, responsibility, or self-sacrifice may have felt overly responsible for family members in their youth. Related thoughts include:

- I have to do everything perfectly
- If I make a mistake, it means I'm careless or a failure, etc.
- If I've done something wrong, I have to make up for it, volunteering or helping others

- It's not okay to ask for help - I always have to be strong/tough
- I have to do everything myself
- If I don't do it, no one will
- I'm responsible for everyone and everything
- If I care enough, I can fix him/her/this
- I can't trust or rely on another person; if I do, they may hurt me (and I won't survive)
- People will betray me - people are not trustworthy
- My needs are not important - I shouldn't spend time taking care of myself
- When I see, that others need help, I have to help them
- I'm only worthwhile if I'm helping other people
- If I express negative feelings in a relationship, terrible things will happen
- I have to make people happy - If people are not happy it's my fault

The above core beliefs and related thoughts represent some common possibilities. Other core beliefs may relate to

- approval-seeking: "I'm only worth something if people like me"
- autonomy: "if someone enters my world, I will have no freedom at all"
- failure: "If I don't succeed, I'm worthless"
- feeling unwanted: "I don't belong anywhere"

etc.

HOW TO APPROACH LIMITING
BELIEFS THE NLP-WAY

"We can't be afraid of change. You may feel very secure in the pond that you are in, but if you never venture out of it, you will never know that there is such a thing as an ocean, a sea. Holding onto something that is good for you now, maybe the very reason why you don't have something better." — C. JoyBell C.

In her book "Stronger Than Circumstances," Mary Morrissey says "Paradigms are the old beliefs that you acquired while you were growing up. They're the habits that protect the status quo, the mindsets that make positive changes feel unfamiliar and uncomfortable, and the fears that tell you that if you try, you will only fail."

If you don't want to work with pre-fabricated beliefs you can use the following form for brainstorming.

What are your old limiting beliefs?

What do you think about…

- Family/Parents/Siblings

  _____

- Relationships/Friendships/Parents/Siblings

  _____

- Love/Kindness/Authenticity

  _____

- Loss/Grief/Trauma

  _____

- Anger/Arguments/Confrontations

  _____

- Challenges/Roadblocks/New Experiences

  _____

- Life/Living

  _____

- Body Image/Weight

  _____

- Cultures/Religion

  _____

After tapping through your OLD beliefs, you may replace them by formulating NEW beliefs as positive affirmations.

For example, if your old belief was "I have inherited obesity from my mother and there's nothing I can do about it." you could replace/rephrase/reframe it with "There's scientific evidence that genetic predisposition is not destiny. Many people who carry so-called "obesity genes" do not become overweight." Hold your ESR points and imagine how you release the old thought through your breath. Your NEW belief could be "I am capable of losing weight easily just by eating a healthy diet, and exercising daily."

In NLP every belief-changing process includes an ecology check. To ensure congruence, it is very important to make sure that all aspects of you are ready for the change. The ecology check invites you to look

- at the impact of the change before making it
- and all the consequences including future actions and plans

from a dissociated objective position.

NLP ECOLOGY CHECK

When you are trying to affect change in your life all parts of your mind must be heading in the same direction. Checking the ecology means that you take every aspect of a possible outcome into account and ensure that it fits in with all aspects of your life.

To check the ecology, you would ask the following questions:

- What is the worst-case scenario that can happen if the OLD belief gets released?

  _____

- What is the worst-case scenario that's possible if the OLD belief is kept?

  _____

- What are the benefits and the very best outcome from changing beliefs that can happen to everyone involved, including the belief holder?

  _____

- What could be a probable loss from letting go of the OLD belief?

  _____

- What would indicate that the NEW belief has been successfully integrated?

  _____

- Is there still (subconscious) resistance on the soul level?

  _____

- Who will be affected negatively by changing the belief?

  _____

- What exactly will change when the NEW belief is adopted?

  _____

- How will daily life look like or be impacted by the NEW belief?

  _____

- What will be the long-term results of the NEW belief?

  _____

- How will certain areas of life change along with the belief change?

  _____

    - Fun and leisure time _____

    - Romance and significant other _____

    - Friends and family _____

    - Finances _____

    - Health & well being _____

    - Personal development _____

    - Career _____

- Will the NEW belief take life to a new level?

  _____

NLP DISNEY STRATEGY FOR INTEGRATING A NEW BELIEF

The original NLP technique is called "Disney Creativity Strategy" and it separates three vital roles for the client – the dreamer, the realist, and the critic. It was created as a simple and efficient approach to identifying the "magical" ideas for business projects.

It was not intended to evaluate and integrate new beliefs, but I always use things differently and enjoy experimenting with energy fields and eye accessing cues. Therefore, I added two more energy fields.

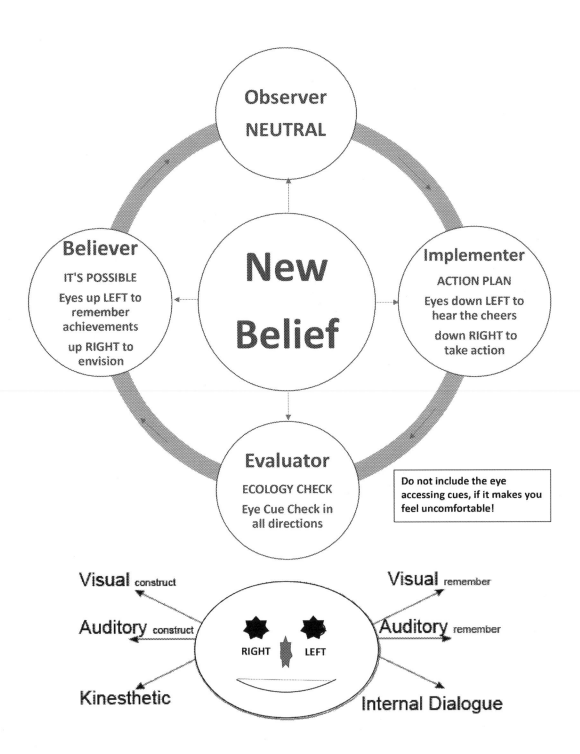

"Disney Strategy" Constellation Work

- Step into field 2 and check how you feel about your new belief. A little bit anxious, wobbly, insecure? (Tap it away)
- Step into field 3. Remember how changing a belief in the past helped you grow and improve your life. Dream big about how integrating this new belief could help you with achievements and success. Dream into the future and see all the possibilities and opportunities. (Tap into Positiveness)
- Step into field 4 and evaluate if anything is holding you back. (Tap away stuckness)
- Step into field 5 and plan the exact next steps you would take with this new belief. (Tap into action)
- Step into field 1 and observe what happened in the three fields around the belief. See everything evolve. See how the person moves, speaks, dresses, and behaves with the new belief. See how this person achieves goals, cheered on by family and friends. (Tap into success)
- Step back into field 2 and check again how you feel about your new belief. Strong, confident, motivated, unstoppable? Congratulations!!!

FIELD 1
OBSERVER
Looking at the picture from an above perspective like an eagle, without emotional involvement

FIELD 2
NEW BELIEF
Formulated in a SMART (goal) way: specific, measurable, achievable, realistic, and timely!

FIELD 3
BELIEVER
Believing that a change of beliefs is possible, open to daring and courageously moving forward

FIELD 4
EVALUATOR
Constructively critical, checking the ecology, weighing cons and pros, presenting what still needs to be released to take the next step with the new belief

- What's the evidence that this belief is true?

- What's the evidence that this belief is false?
- Is this belief rather a habit than a fact?
- Is the interpretation of the belief objective or subjective?
- Is the belief generalized or reflects black and white categories? (I always.../If I can't... I'm a failure)
- Was the belief-causing situation taken out of context and only one aspect of the whole taken into consideration?
- Is the SOURCE (parent/caregiver etc.) of the belief reliable?
- Is there sufficient **evidence** or justification to support the belief?

FIELD 5
IMPLEMENTER
Taking the input of the evaluator and turning strategy into action

I used to create energy fields with ropes, hoops, or pieces of paper. Now, I use a Lenormand card deck with its universal symbols that everyone can decipher and read.

Let's look at an example:
Old belief: I don't think I'm the type of person who would be able to make a lot of money because...

New belief: I am worthy and deserving of money, wealth, and financial success as a result of having added value to other people's lives.

- First, we would check the new belief with muscle testing to find out the percentage of motivation (0-100%).
- Then, we would tap on the old belief and find out what's coming up from the past to get rid of.
- Next, we would do another tapping round on the old belief, opening up for possibilities ("what-if" tapping).
- Finally, we would tap on the new belief, including the 9-Gamut Procedure, to integrate it completely.
- The Motivation Check would decide about our next step. If the motivation is 100%, we wouldn't have to do anything but celebrate.
- However, if it's still under 100% I would start the constellation (Disney strategy see above).

- Sometimes the cards tell us already what to work on in the different fields.
- Sometimes I muscle-test the Emotion Code (I have created a short version of it, later on in the book), to find out if the trapped emotion is linked to the belief we're currently working on and whether it is pre-conceptional, prenatal, natal, from one's own life experience, inherited/ancestral, from a past life, generational or from the vast energy field of collective cosmic consciousness.

Then I would ask if I needed to know more, like who was involved. Most of the time this is a "no" anyway and so, I may help my client to release the stuck emotion for good. I usually hold the ESR points, connect with the Superconscious Oneness and I often feel a subtle movement of the head when the trauma gets released.

The **Cartesian Coordinates** can also be applied when it comes to checking the ecology and whether the outcome of the NEW belief is worth pursuing.

- If I do this, what will happen?
- If I do this, what won't happen?
- If I don't do this, what will happen?
- If I don't do this, what won't happen?

USING THE MAGIC WAND TO EVALUATE YOUR NEW BELIEF

If you are more of a creative person who doesn't want to evaluate and analyze facts, there's always the famous "Magic Wand" exercise with 8 important questions. I would recommend recording the questions with your voice recorder and leaving at least three minutes after each question, so you can close your eyes and connect to your inner wisdom.

If you could wave a magic wand, how would everything around you change? What would happen if you erased your outdated belief and replaced it with a new one that's encouraging, inspiring, and motivating?

- How would your life change?

  _____

- How would you change?

  _____

- What would you feel?

  _____

- How would you move?

  _____

  Go ahead and MOVE! Straight posture? Tall and confident? Grounded and connected?

- What would you hear?

  _____

- What would you see?

  _____

- What would you taste?

  _____

- What would you smell?

  _____

This exercise is not just used by counselors, it's also part of NLP (Neuro-Linguistic Programing).

For each of our memories, there's a unique set of submodalities, the combination of which gets used internally to represent that memory. Submodalities are part of our very complex internal representation system we can access. This means, that if we change the submodalities, we change the internal representation, which in turn changes the meaning, which then will also result in a change of behavior. Submodalities are the fine details of each SENSE (visual, auditory, gustatory, olfactory, kinesthetic) or modality.

And don't forget to check your answers with muscle testing. If you feel any incongruence or resistance immediately tap on the side of your hand to remove subconscious self-sabotage.

Remember, any pre-made script will never be able to replace a session with an expert because it will never be specific enough and won't touch all layers that have to be peeled. However, it may remove some subconscious blockages and it will most definitely relax you.

TAPPING SCRIPT FOR FEAR OF CHANGE

Rate your fear of change on a scale of 0-10

SOH: Even though I'm scared of feeling out of control unless my life remains the same, I deeply and completely love, accept and forgive myself.

Even though I don't feel capable of making the right decision when it comes to changing directions in my life, I deeply and completely love, accept and forgive myself.

Even though I feel ungrateful and unworthy of earning more money or finding the perfect partner or … (just fill in what comes to mind), I deeply and completely love, accept and forgive myself.

1. Round

IE: I'm scared of any change

OE: I'm scared of feeling overwhelmed and out of control

UE: I'm scared of making mistakes.

N&C: I'm scared of making wrong decisions.

C&N: I'm so scared that I'm not good enough to deserve better.

H&H: I'm so scared of being rejected if I change my belief

H&H: I'm so scared that because of my upbringing and my family roots I will never be successful

Liver: I'm scared that I'm not smart enough and don't have the credentials to be successful

UA: I'm scared that there's something wrong with me because I feel that nothing seems to work out in my life

2. Round

IE: Fact is, that I won't be able to avoid change entirely

OE: There are tools I can learn to avoid overwhelm and anxiety, and the fact is, that some things in life cannot be controlled

UE: Fact is, that everyone makes mistakes and even the most famous inventors had to experiment to see what works

N&C: The fact is, wrong decisions create an enormous potential for learning and self-development

C&N: Many people don't feel good enough, but everyone has a CHOICE to learn how to be self-confident

H&H: There is no proof that I will be rejected and maybe I will get to know interesting people and make new friends

H&H: Some very famous people had a difficult or even abusive upbringing, broke free and became very successful

Liver: There are people without high school diplomas who became famous and millionaires

UA: I know that life is not a bed of roses, neither for me nor for everyone else.

3. Round

IE: What if I accepted that there's a need for change to see the vast ocean of possibilities

OE: What if I could deal with the anxiety and overwhelm connected to change and life challenges

UE: What if I could see that every change just gets me closer to my dreams

N&C: What if I could develop more self-confidence and courage to take a leap

C&N: What if I could start with a little change to my daily routines

H&H: What if I just stayed present and just took one step at a time

H&H: What if I could move freely if I released my inner child from the prison of the past

Liver: What if I could find the spark inside of me that ignites my zeal to move beyond what I ever thought possible

Put your hands in a prayer position, take six deep breaths and compare your numbers on a scale from 0-10 before and after tapping.

CORE CAUSES WORKSHEET

While tapping on the side of your hand (formerly called "karate chop") to remove resistance and invite trauma to the surface, explore areas of your life, core beliefs, and trapped emotions.

What is your issue? Choose ONLY ONE specific issue at a time! And remember, you can always muscle test and ask, "What area am I supposed to work with today/right now?"

o   Relationship

_____

o   Sexuality

_____

o   Workplace – Job – Business

_____

o   Financial Challenges

_____

o   Peak Performance – Success

_____

o   Life Purpose – Calling – Meaning

_____

o   Life Transitions – Life Changes

_____

o   Health – Certain Pain – Organs (physical area)

_____

o   Grief – Loss (health, work, pet, loved one)

_____

o   Other

_____

_____

_____

CHAPTER THREE

COLLECTION OF EMOTIONAL RELEASE TECHNIQUES WORKBOOK

- Release Of Trapped Emotions – MY Version Of The Emotion Code
- My Daily Ritual
- Synesthesia
- Jin Shin Jyutsu Finger Hold
- Brazilian Toe Technique
- Ho'oponopono – The Hawaiian Way Of Healing
- Ho'oponopono & EFT Tapping
- Balancing The Seven Chakras – Reflective Questions
- The Seven Chakras With Mudras & Mantras
- EFT Tapping For Balancing The Chakras With Affirmations
- Bach Flowers – Overview & List For Muscle Testing
- EFT Tapping With Bach Flower Affirmations
- The Sedona Method
- EFT Tapping With The Sedona Method

What are the trapped emotions associated with your issue? (All emotions, besides affecting the organ directly, affect the Heart indirectly because the Heart houses the Mind.)

A	Stomach	→ Worry	→ Nervousness, Anxiety, Despair, Disgust
	Spleen	→ Low Self-Esteem	→ Lack Of Control, Hopelessness, Helplessness, Failure
B	Kidney	→ Fear	→ Horror, Dread, Blame, Annoyance
	Bladder	→ Conflict	→ Terror, No Support, Spine/Gutlessness, Creative Insecurity
C	Liver	→ Anger	→ Hatred, Resentment, Bitterness, Guilt
	Gallbladder	→ Indecisiveness	→ Taken For Granted, Frustration, Panic, Depression
D	Lungs	→ Grief	→ Despair, Sadness, Sorrow, Discouragement
	Large Intestine	→ Rejection	→ Defensiveness, Confusion, Self-Abuse, Stubbornness
E	Heart	→ Overjoy	→ Abandonment, Heartache, Betrayal, Forlorn
	Small Intestine	→ Effort Unreceived	→ Love Unreceived, Lost, Vulnerability, Insecurity
F	Triple Warmer	→ Humiliation	→ Shock, Overwhelm, Jealousy, Unworthy
	Pericardium	→ Shame	→ Lust, Longing, Aversion, Fear Of Intimacy
	(Circulation Sex)		

You can work with the Trapped Emotions Paragraph on its own. And some of you might be reminded of "The Emotion Code" by Dr. Nelson.

I would like to quote him here to explain this subconscious phenomenon: "Trapped emotions are truly an invisible epidemic in our world. As we go through our lives, we experience different emotions all the time, which is completely normal. Sometimes, however, we experience very negative emotions such as anger, frustration, resentment, sorrow, sadness, and so on. Every emotion has a certain frequency or vibration. When we are feeling an intense emotion, the energy of that emotion can become trapped in the body.

Trapped emotions can occur at any age and they can even be inherited. They can cause inflammation, congestion, self-sabotage, depression, anxiety, and relationship difficulties. When an emotion gets trapped in the body you will continue to feel that emotion. For instance, if you have a trapped emotion of anger, you will find yourself becoming angry much more readily than you normally would. Why? Because part of you is already vibrating at that frequency.

When we find and release a trapped emotion, often we see an immediate healing effect as the body is allowed to return to its normal, healthy, undisturbed state. When this happens, we know we have gotten to the root cause of the illness." ~*Dr. Bradley Nelson*

I practice releasing trapped emotions daily, mostly in the morning after waking up.

This is my very own ritual:

1. **I set my intentions for the day:**

SOH: I attract health, wealth, abundance, and personal growth in all areas of life like work, finances, relationships, family, etc.

IE: What's meant for me will find me.

OE: As I am at peace. Only positive energy will come my way.

UE: I align myself with all things meant for my greater good.

N&C: I am grateful for all the joy, abundance, and love that finds me today.

C&N: I am open to receiving love.

Kidney: I let go of what no longer serves me.

UC: I have the power to create my life, my emotions, my thoughts, and my behaviors.

UA: And I claim this power now. I am always guided toward my purpose.

H&H: Love and money come to me easily today.

H&H: I am ready to receive abundance and miracles.

3rdE: I have it within me to solve any challenges that come my way.

Heart Prayer Position: 6 deep breaths

2. **I ask if there is there anything that needs to be cleared up right now before I can start the new day, living the best version I can be.**

- I ask: Do I have a trapped feeling, thought, or soul contract that is best to be cleared, healed, and released right now?
- I ask: Is it in A, B, C, D, E, F?
- Let's say, it is B. I ask: Is it an energy blockage in the Kidney Meridian? In the Bladder Meridian?
- Let's say, it is in the Kidney Meridian. I know today's topic is fear. I ask: Is it Horror, Dread, Blame, Annoyance?
- Let's say it's Horror. I ask: Can I release the emotional energy blockage now? Do I need to know more?
- Let's say, I need to know more. I ask: Does the energy blockage come from…
  o past lives,

- o parents,
- o ancestors,
- o conception concepts,
- o problems during birth,
- o decisions, attitudes, alignments, truths, contracts, oaths, agreements, vows, unresolved thoughts, thought patterns,
- o metaphors & beliefs
- o the collective field
- Let's say my muscle test says "yes" to problems during birth and metaphors & beliefs, and I know that my mother almost died at birth. My subconscious belief might be "I almost killed my mother. I have no right to be here." If this popped up, I ask: "Is this what has to be released now?"
- When I get a yes, I ask again: can I release it now? When I get a yes again, I hold the ESR points and breathe deeply until I feel a release.
- Show gratitude! "Great Spirit and Spirit Guides, please fill all voids with Your LOVE and LIGHT to heal completely and wholly, so that I can become the true me, I am meant to be. Thank You! Thank you! Thank you!"

What does a release feel like? How do you know you have released the trapped emotion for good? First of all, when it is released, you can't find it anymore. Often, during the release, you feel a little confused or dizzy, or you feel sensations or a subtle motion in your body.

When I hold the ESR points on the head of my client often their head starts to move, and I follow the motion. I had one client who almost fell backward into my arms during the release.

3. **What's your negative "self-talk" about the issue?**
   (Choose from this list or Core Limiting Beliefs)

- o I'm not good enough
- o I'm stupid
- o It's impossible to heal
- o I don't have what it takes
- o What will they think?
- o I'm scared to fail, I'm a born loser
- o If I'm successful people will hate me
- o Rich people are greedy
- o I'm afraid of responsibility

o   I will lose love, appreciation, and attention
o   I will never be able to trust again
o   I am unworthy of love
o   In the end, I'm left alone
o   I'm not ready yet
o   Nobody helps me!
o   I'm too proud to ask for help
o   I have to do it by myself
o   I'm unattractive
o   I'm TOO …
o   I should have … (but now it's too late).
o   Life is not fair to me.
o   I don't deserve …
o   I'm afraid of being seen
o   I can't be heard
o   I'll be punished
o   I'm the victim!
o   I will never forgive...
o   My needs don't matter
o   I'm a burden
o   Everything is out of my control
o   Life is too hard
o   I'll never succeed.
o   I don't deserve happiness.
o   I'm stuck forever...
o   I just want to die.
o   Other (please specify) _____

_____

_____

4.   **What beliefs did you learn during your upbringing? (Example: "If you don't go to church you'll burn in hell.")**

Please specify: _____

_____

5. **Who do you blame or hold responsible for this issue, (even if it's not their fault)?**

   o   Myself
   o   (Step) Mother or (Step) Father
   o   Sister(s) / Brother(s) / Cousins
   o   Grandma or Grandpa
   o   Aunt or Uncle
   o   Friend(s) / Neighbors
   o   Child Care
   o   Teacher / Coach
   o   Religion / Church / God
   o   Husband / Wife
   o   Child / Children
   o   Society / Mentality
   o   Karma

6. **Who in your family modeled similar attitudes and feelings? (Could you have picked up or inherited feelings, thoughts, and beliefs from someone you were around as a child?) One of your:**

   o   (Step) Parents / Grandparents / Relatives / Caregivers
   o   (Step) Sibling(s)
   o   Other (please specify) _____

   _____

   _____

7. **Where do you feel this in your body? (For example, it may be pressure in your head or tension in your stomach.)**

   o   My entire body
   o   Head
   o   Face
   o   Eyes
   o   Ears

o   Neck
o   Throat
o   Shoulders
o   Arms
o   Hands
o   Chest
o   Heart
o   Back
o   Stomach
o   Hips
o   Legs
o   Knees
o   Other (please specify) _____

_____

_____

8. **If you were to describe the emotion or pain in your body, what would be the...**

Shape (round, square etc.) _____

Size (small, big etc.) _____

Texture (soft, rough etc.) _____

Color (one or multi-colored) _____

Temperature (hot, cold etc.) _____

Motion or Stillness (fast, slow etc.) _____

Sound, Smell or Taste (sweet, sour, loud, quiet etc.) _____

Other: _____

Synesthesia is a technique that is best done in a light trance.

In this technique, you explore pain as a sensation. What exactly is the pain? Where is it, is it a slow or a fast-moving pain? Does it have any color and texture? How does it move?

Try and put some meaning to your pain, give it shape so that it makes some sense to your unconscious mind.

The next step is to imagine that the pain is outside your body where it is easier to observe. Try and examine it from a distance of about two meters.

Now you can change the quality of pain. Make it smaller or bigger or change the color and the sound. Change the way it moves and observe what happens.

Finally, when you are satisfied with the changes you have made, you can send your pain to a faraway place, or you can just turn it upside down and put it back in the same place so that it cancels out the original pain.

9. **What benefit(s) do you think you receive by holding on to this issue?**

    o   Protection from hurt
    o   Teaching "them" a lesson
    o   Punishing myself
    o   My suffering hurts "them"
    o   Proving something
    o   Attention/Love/Worthiness
    o   Other (please specify) _____

    _____

Self-Sabotaging Reasons:

*   **FEAR:** of the change = unknown, of affecting relationships, of getting hurt, of regret, etc.
*   **RESISTANCE:** to forming new habits, giving up old habits, getting uncomfortable, etc.
*   **DOUBT:** that you can do it & keep it up, that you are worth it, that you'll be accepted etc.

Your subconscious truly believes it's helping you by resisting you to change! It prefers to stay with what's familiar because at least it knows how to keep you safe in this comfort zone (that's not comfortable at all!). So, it's pulling you back when you get closer to your desired goal to protect you from that danger.

10. **How would this issue, pain, or belief look like if you'd created a picture/collage of it? (Our first Expressive Arts Exercise: use wax or chalk crayons or watercolors on white or black paper)**

Give it a shape (abstract or concrete), object, or geometric design, whatever comes into your mind first. Is it black and white or color, small or large, just a scribble, some doodling?

JIN SHIN JYUTSU FINGER HOLD

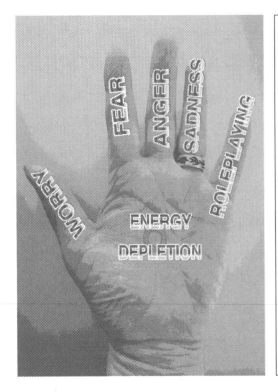

Thumb   WORRY - (Stomach/Spleen)
"I'm at peace & filled with confidence"
Index Finger   FEAR - (Kidney/Bladder)
"I let my light shine bright and love will set me free!"
Middle Finger   ANGER - (Liver/Gallbladder)
"I see clearly and hear the guidance of my inner voice" **"I'm able to forgive"**
Ring Finger   SADNESS /GRIEF - (Lungs/Colon)
"I breathe DEEPLY & fill my lungs with joy"
Little Finger   CONTROL/ROLES – (Heart/Small Intest.)
"Now I let go and let Life flow"

By holding each thumb and finger, in turn, every day for a few minutes, we can calm the mind, soothe the nervous system, and regenerate our whole being.

Brazilian Toe Technique

uses acupressure points to promote deep relaxation and activates the release of toxins. This simple method can help reduce emotional stress, imbalances, overall physical pain, achiness. It also reduces the side effects of chemotherapy/radiation, restless leg syndrome, insomnia, nausea, and edema.

1) Place your thumbs beneath their middle toes and your middle fingers on top of the same toes, on the toenails. Hold lightly for 2-3 minutes. Breathe in through your nose and out through your mouth.

2) Slide your thumbs to the bottom of their fourth toes, then slide your fourth (or ring) fingers on top of the fourth toes. Hold lightly for two to three minutes. Continue the same breathing.

3) Slide your thumbs beneath the little toes, then slide your little fingers on top of the toenails. Hold lightly for two to three minutes.

4) Slide your thumbs beneath the second toes, then slide your index fingers on top of the toenails of their second toes. Hold lightly for two to three minutes.

5) Slide your thumbs beneath their big toes, then place your index and middle fingers so that one is on each side of the base of the toenails of the big toes. Hold lightly for two to three minutes.

HO'OPONOPONO, THE HAWAIIAN PRAYER OF LOVE, FORGIVENESS, AND GRATITUDE

The practice of ho'oponopono is to take absolute responsibility for "SELF" and all you perceive and react to as "SELF", whether this is something personally distressing or something you are reacting to in another – in Ho'oponopono all is "SELF", there is no separation so there can be no blame.

ALIGNMENT PROCEDURE by Brian Gerard Schaefer

1. **Establish a Divine Connection**
   - Stand in solitude before the Source – in absolute stillness, emptiness, silence, solitude
   - Experience the Divine Nature – Oneness, Bliss, and Immortality
   - Feel the purity and intensity of the Divine Love and Light
   - Sense Oneness with the Omnipotence, Omniscience, and Omnipresence of the Source

2. **Establish a True relationship with Creation**
   - Establish a True connection to the Unity within the Diversity of the Universal Form
   - Establish a True relationship with all things at the point of your/our collective Mergence
   - Honour the Evolution of Consciousness – total ignorance to full awareness of the Divine Nature
   - Honour the Universal Plan unfolding – the inevitability and effortlessness towards Mergence
   - Honour the Play of Consciousness – the appearance of duality/individuality - separation/ division
   - Honour the Divine Elements at work in, through, and around all Forms/Beings, in all worlds

3. **Establish Empowerment**
   - Be a pure instrument of the Divine Elements
   - Maintain the connection to the Divine Presence within all Forms of Being
   - Affirm your and their worthiness, deservedness, right, permission to be at One with the Source
   - Establish your Heavenly relationship with another Form/Being, looking back to your time on Earth and your ability to put back whatever was missing

72

4. **Establish a connection to Nature**
   - Honour the Earth/ Realm, Nature, and the Universal Form
   - Honour all the Laws that determine Evolution and Flow on Earth and in the human experience

Greater power is given to any prayers when you speak the words out loud. And you can tap along:

Opening Prayer "I" AM THE "I"

SOH:	*"I" come forth from the void into the light.*
IE:	*"I" am the breath that nurtures life.*
OE:	*"I" am that emptiness, that hollowness, beyond all consciousness.*
UE:	*The "I" the Identity, the ALL*
N&C:	*"I" draw my bow of rainbows across the waters,*
C&N:	*…the continuum of minds with matters*
CB:	*"I" am incoming and outgoing of breath.*
H&H:	*The invisible, untouchable breeze*
H&H:	*The undefinable atom of creation*

Healing Prayer Position: "I" AM THE "I" – "I" LOVES ME and take 6 deep breaths

Uhane – the Conscious Mind – the MOTHER

The reasonable mind is ruled by logic. It believes that it solves problems and controls what it experiences and what happens. The Hawaiians know that we are not solely our intellect or Conscious Mind. The Conscious Mind and the Unconscious mind are collectively known as the soul.

Unihipili – the Unconscious Mind. – the CHILD

The Unconscious Mind controls the functions of the physical body. (In Western science this is recognized as control through the autonomic nervous system.) The Hawaiian systems of healing acknowledged the equal importance of each mind. Being connected to and trusting one's Unconscious Mind is a very important element of their system. This would be akin to trusting one's intuition or gut reaction.

Aumakua -the Higher Conscious Mind – the FATHER

The Hawaiians believe that we are created equally of matter and spirit, rather like a magnet – with one aspect manifested in matter and another in spirit. Both aspects are connected by an unseen force or energy called Mana. The Higher Conscious Mind is always connected to Divinity.

The Higher Conscious is a mind of eternal light, the all-knowing intelligence of the soul.

Peace Prayer

SOH: Spirit, Higher (Super) Conscious Mind, if I, my family, relatives, and ancestors have offended you... your family, relatives, and ancestors in thought, words, deeds, and actions from the beginning of our creation to the present, humbly we ask you all for forgiveness for all our fears, errors, resentments, guilt, offenses, blocks, and attachments we have created, accumulated and accepted from the beginning of our creation to the present

3rd Eye: Let the Higher Conscious Mind (Superconscious/Divine Intelligence) include all pertinent information we knowingly or unknowingly have omitted.

IE: Will you all forgive us.
OE: Yes, we forgive you.

UE: Let the water of life release us all from spiritual, mental, physical, material, financial and karmic bondage.

N&C: Pull out of our memory bank and computer, release and sever and cut the unwanted and/or negative data, memories, and blocks that tie, bind and attach us.

C&N: Cleanse, purify and transmute all these unwanted energies to Pure Light.

CB: Fill the spaces these unwanted energies occupied with Divine light

H&H: Let divine order, light, love, peace, balance, wisdom, understanding, and abundance be made manifest for us all in our affairs through the divine power of the divine creator, father-mother-child as one in whom we rest, abide, and have our being now and forevermore.

H&H: We are set free, and it is done

Ho'oponopono Prayer – Healing Position:

IE: I am responsible for...

OE: Please forgive me.

UE: I am sorry.

UN: I love you.

CH: Thank you.

CB: Please forgive me.

H&H: I love you.

H&H: Thank you.

The Ho'oponopono prayer for cleaning is a gift that was given freely to the world by Morrnah Simeona. It will bring you greater peace within all areas of your life. Morrnah recommended that whatever issue you are working on, the prayer should be recited four times, speaking the words out loud.

Cleaning-Releasing Prayer

SOH: Spirit, Superconscious, please locate the origin of my feelings, thoughts of .... (issue).

3rdE: Take every level, layer, area, and aspect of my being to this origin.

OE: Analyse and resolve it perfectly with God's Truth.

UE: Come through all generations of time and eternity.

N&C: Healing every incident and its appendages based on the origin.

C&N: Please do it according to God's Will until I am at the present, filled with light and truth.

K: God's Peace and Love, Forgiveness of myself for my incorrect perceptions.

Wrist: Forgiveness of every person, place, circumstances, and events which contributed to this, these feelings and thoughts.

SOH: Spirit, Superconscious, if I, my family, relatives, and ancestors have offended you in thoughts, words, deeds, and actions from the beginning of our creation to the present, please forgive us.

3rdE: Cleanse, purify, release, sever and cut all the unwanted energies and vibrations we have created, accumulated, and/or accepted from the beginning of our creation to the present.

SOE: Please transmute all the negative, unwanted energies to Pure Light.

UE: We are set free!

N&C   and it is done (let go and let God)

Heart Prayer Position – Take 6 deep breaths – 1 I'm sorry – 2 Please forgive me – 3 I love you – 4 Thank you – 5 Peace begins with me – 6 Namaste, OM

Ho'oponopono Prayer Statements:

I'm sorry - ACKNOWLEDGEMENT

Humbleness. Simply state and own the problem. Acknowledging the problem. A profound softening and kindness to the self (and others as self).

Please forgive me - FORGIVENESS

Acknowledging responsibility – absolute – it exists in my life, in my world, therefore I caused it, breathed it into being. Now it can be released

I Love You - LOVE

This is a state we sink into. Focus on the heart – breathe in love, breathe out love. Love is the form of the Divine. Love alone can merge in love. When we are filled with Divine Love, we can experience Oneness and offer our problems to divinity to dissolve.

Thank you - GRATITUDE

Thank you for the healing. Thank you for all that the problem has given me (even if I cannot see/know what this is right now). Thank you for what it may have taught me. Breathe in, focus your attention on your heart as you feel gratitude, and breathe out from the heart as you think about gratitude.

Ho'oponopono means "to make right", "to rectify an error" or "correct the wrongs" that had occurred.

Effectively, it means to make it right with the ancestors, your family, friends, or anyone or anything with whom or which you have a relationship. This can include animals, vegetables or minerals and indeed our planet.

Na kala is the Fortune of Forgiveness

Hawaiian values include a profound code of forgiveness. They believe that when we forgive others, we are also forgiving ourselves.

Kala means "to untie, unbind and set free." The person, group, or nation to whom the wrongdoer is indebted free themselves and the 'others' of the karmic debt or wrongdoing. It does not exist anymore. This could only be done by unbinding attachments to the past wrongs; by making right the future.

Other healing traditions have similar teachings. For instance, in Neuro-Linguistic Programming (NLP), there is a saying, "People do the best they can with the resources they have available." This is a forgiveness concept – especially when you include yourself as one of those "people."

Contrary to Western therapy, in Ho'oponopono, the therapist comes from the position of having created the issue, and not the client. In Dr. Ihaleakala Hew Len's approach, it is the therapist's responsibility to help clients in working through their issues. He states that "the therapist must be willing to be 100% responsible for having created the problem situation, that is, he must be willing to see that the source of the problem is erroneous thoughts within him, not within the client. Therapists never seem to notice that every time there is a problem, they are always present!"

BALANCING THE SEVEN CHAKRAS

Chakra translates to "wheel" (wheel of spinning energy/vortex) in Sanskrit. The body contains seven energy centers, known as chakras. Together, these energy centers are an archetypal depiction of your individual maturation through seven distinct stages.

The direction in which the chakras rotate is also different in the two sexes making them unique to their gender. The male and female chakra systems are the manifestation of Shiva and Shakti, their heaven-bound counterparts.

Chakras that move clockwise spin the energy out (positive pole/giving) and chakras that spin counterclockwise pull energy in (negative pole/receiving).

The odd chakras – 1st, 3rd, and 5th – are "masculine" YANG (penetrative) by nature.

- (1st-Root Chakra): grounding/stability
- (3rd-Solar Chakra): action/power
- (5th-Throat Chakra): purpose/expression

The even chakras – 2nd, 4th, and 6th – are "feminine" YIN (receptive) by nature.

- (2nd-Sacral Chakra): intimacy/surrender to life's flow
- (4th-Heart Chakra): love/compassion
- (6th-Brow Chakra): insight/intuition

The 7th chakra is gender-neutral – Higher Conscious

1. First Chakra – Muladhara, Base or Root Chakra

My Roots or Where I Come From (biological, ancestral, generational, collective)

Giving mode in Male Body - Receiving Mode in Female body – 1-7 years

Mantra: I AM – deeply rooted   **Color: Red**   **Element: Earth**   **Stone: Hematite**

Physical family and group safety and security, ability to provide for life's necessities and stand up for yourself, feeling at home, social and familial law and order, abandonment fears, family bonding, identity, tribal honor code, support, and loyalty.

Self-Examination by Caroline Myss

1. What belief patterns did you inherit from your family?

    _____

2. Do all of them still have authority over you?

    _____

3. What superstitions do you have? Which have more authority over you than your own reasoning ability?

    _____

4. Do you have a personal code of honor? What is it?

    _____

5. Have you ever compromised your sense of honor? If so, have you taken steps to heal it?

    _____

6. Do you have any unfinished business with your family members? Resistance to healing it?

    _____

7. List all the blessings that you feel come from your family.

    _____

8. If you are a parent, what qualities would you like your children to learn from you?

    _____

9. What tribal traditions and rituals do you continue?

    _____

10. What tribal characteristics within yourself would you like to strengthen and develop?

    _____

2. Second Chakra – Swadhisthana, Sacral, or Navel Chakra
Relationships – I & Others

Giving mode in Female Body - Receiving Mode in Male body – 8-14 years

Mantra: I FEEL – connected   **Color: Orange**   **Element: Water**   **Stone: Tiger's Eye**

Fear of loss of control, through events such as addiction, rape, betrayal, impotence, financial loss, or abandonment by partners or colleagues, ability to take risks, personal identity, blame, guilt, money, sex, power, control, creativity, ethics, honor in relationships, decision-making ability, power to rebel.

Self-Examination by Caroline Myss

1. How do you define creativity? Do you consider yourself a creative person? Do you follow through on your creative ideas?

    _____

2. Do you often direct your creative energies into negative paths of expression? Do you exaggerate or embellish "facts" to support your point of view?

    _____

3. Are you comfortable with your sexuality? If not, are you working toward healing your sexual imbalances? Do you use people for sexual pleasure, or have you felt used? Do you honor your own sexual boundaries?

    _____

4. Do you keep your word? What is your personal code of ethics? Do you negotiate your ethics depending on your circumstances?

    _____

5. Do you have an impression of the Divine as a force that exerts justice in your life?

    _____

3. Third Chakra – Manipura, or Solar Plexus Chakra
   I & My Divinity

Giving mode in Male Body - Receiving Mode in Female body – 15-21 years

Mantra: I DO – with who I am & I deeply and completely appreciate myself for who I am

Color: Yellow/Gold   Element: Fire   Stone: Amber

Trust, fear, intimidation, self-esteem, self-confidence, self-respect, ambition, courage, ability to handle a crisis, care of yourself and others, sensitivity to criticism, personal honor, fear of rejection and looking foolish, physical appearance anxieties, strength of character.

Self-Examination by Caroline Myss

1. Do you like yourself? What don't you like and why? Are you actively working to change the things about yourself you don't like?

   _____

2. Are you honest? Do you sometimes misrepresent the truth? Why?

   _____

3. Are you critical of others? Do you blame others as a way of protecting yourself?

   _____

4. Are you able to admit when you are wrong? Are you open to feedback from other people about yourself?

   _____

5. Do you need the approval of others? If so, why?

   _____

4. Forth Chakra – Anahata or Heart Chakra
Love - Highest Divine Frequency

Giving mode in Female Body - Receiving Mode in Male body – 21-28 years

Mantra: I LOVE – with all my heart & I deeply and completely love and forgive myself

Color: Green   Element: Air   Stone: Rose Quartz

Love, hatred, bitterness, grief, anger, jealousy, inability to forgive, self-centeredness, fears of loneliness, commitment and betrayal, compassion, hope trust, ability to heal yourself and others.

Self-Examination by Caroline Myss

1. What emotional memories do you still need to heal?

    _____

2. What relationships in your life require healing?

    _____

3. Do you ever use emotional wounds to control people or situations? If so, describe them.

    _____

4. Have you allowed yourself to be controlled by the wounds of another? Will you let that happen again? What steps are you prepared to take to prevent yourself from being controlled that way again?

    _____

5. What fears do you have about becoming emotionally healthy?

    _____

6. Do you associate emotional health with no longer needing an intimate relationship?

_____

7. What is your understanding of forgiveness?

_____

8. Who are the people you need to forgive, and what prevents you from letting go of the pain you associate with them?

_____

5. Fifth Chakra –Vishuddha or Throat Chakra
Willpower - Express Yourself – Voice Your Truth

Giving mode in Male Body - Receiving Mode in Female body – 29-35 years

Mantra: I speak – my truth, always & I fully express myself

Color: Cyan/Turquoise   Element: Sound/Vibration   Stone: Aquamarine

Choice and strength of will, personal expression, following your dreams, using personal power to create, addiction, judgment, criticism, faith, knowledge, capacity to make decisions.

Self-Examination by Caroline Myss

1. What is your definition of being "strong-willed"?

    _____

2. Who are the people that have control over your willpower, and why?

    _____

3. Do you seek to control others? If so, who are they, and why do you need to control them?

    _____

4. Can you express yourself honestly and openly when you need to? If not, why not?

    _____

5. Are you able to sense when you are receiving guidance to act upon?

    _____

6. Do you trust guidance that has no "proof" of the outcome attached to it?

    _____

7. What fears do you have about divine guidance?

   _____

8. Do you pray for assistance with your personal plans, or are you able to say, "I will do what heaven directs me to do"?

   _____

9. What makes you lose control of your own willpower?

   _____

10. Do you know you need to change but continually postpone taking action? If so, identify those situations and your reasons for not acting.

   _____

6. Sixth Chakra –Ajna or Third Eye Chakra
I Follow My Intuition & Trust My Invisible Guidance

Giving mode in Female Body - Receiving Mode in Male body – 36-42 years

Mantra: I see - within & I am open to exploring what cannot be seen.

Color: Midnight Blue   Element: Light   Stone: Amethyst

Self-evaluation, truth, intellectual abilities, feelings of inadequacy, openness to the ideas of others, ability to learn from experience, emotional intelligence.

Self-Examination by Caroline Myss

1. Do you often negatively interpret the actions of others? If so, why?

_____

2. What negative patterns continually surface in your relationships with others?

_____

3. What attitudes do you have that disempower you? What beliefs/attitudes in yourself would you like to change? Can you commit to making those changes?

_____

4. What beliefs do you continue to accept that you know are not true?

_____

5. Are you judgmental? If so, what situations or relationships bring out that tendency?

_____

6. Do you make excuses for behaving in negative ways?

_____

7. Recall instances in which a more profound level of truth than you were used to hearing was revealed. Was the experience intimidating?

_____

8. Are you comfortable thinking about your life in impersonal terms?

_____

9. Do you know you need to change but continually postpone taking action? Identify those situations and your reasons for not acting?

_____

7. Seventh Chakra – Sahasrara, Crown Chakra, or 1000 Petal Lotus
I Am Here & Now – I Am Connected To The All-Knowing Field

Giving mode in Female Body - Receiving Mode in Male body – 43-49 years

Mantra: I understand – Being & I am a vessel for Love & Light

Color: Violet/White   **Element: Divine Conscious**   **Stone: Clear Quartz**

Ability to trust life, values, ethics, courage, humanitarianism, selflessness, ability to see the larger pattern, faith, inspiration, spirituality, and devotion.

Self-Examination by Caroline Myss

1. What guidance have you sought during meditation or praying?

\
\

2. What type of guidance do you fear the most?

\
\

3. Do you bargain with the Divine? Do you complain more than you express gratitude?

\
\

4. Are you devoted to a particular spiritual path? If not, do you feel the need to find one?

\
\

5. Do you believe that your God is more authentic than the Divine in other spiritual traditions?

\
\

6. How would your life change if the Divine answered your questions by saying: "I have no intention of giving you insight at this point in your life"? What would you do then?

\
\

7. Have you started and stopped a meditation practice? If so, what are the reasons that you failed to maintain it?

    _____

8. What spiritual truths are you aware of that you do not live by? List them.

    _____

9. Are you afraid of a closer relationship with the Divine because of changes it might trigger in your life?

    _____

CHAKRAS, MANTRAS & MUDRAS

A **MUDRA** is a sacred and symbolic gesture. Mudras are used as a means of channeling the flow of vital life force energy known as *prana*. The term translates from Sanskrit as "gesture," "mark" or "seal".

The position of our hands has the ability to influence the energy of our physical, emotional, and spiritual bodies. Mudras help to link the brain to the body, soothe pain, stimulate endorphins, change the mood and increase our vitality.

Each individual mudra has unique symbolism and is thought to have a specific effect on the body and mind by clearing energetic pathways. Mudras allow us to go inward and recharge our energy levels.

A **MANTRA** is a word, sound, or phrase repeated to aid in your concentration while meditating. When using a mantra, it's believed that only the positive intentions and actions will fill your mind and eliminate negativity.

A mantra can be as simple as the word 'love,' something you are thankful for, or a phrase such as 'om Shanti, Shanti, Shanti which represents all-encompassing peace. You can also meditate on an affirmation, such as 'I accept myself.'

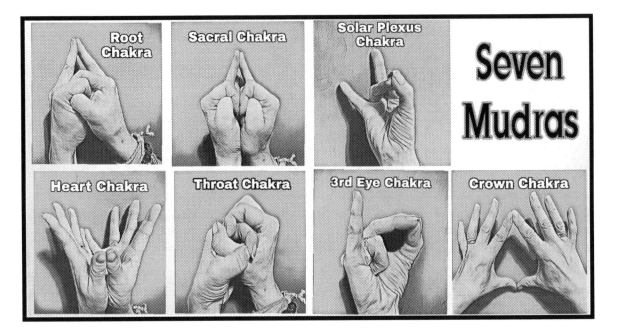

Root Chakra   Mantra LAM

Mudra: Bring your palms together in a prayer at your heart, then interlace the pinky and ring fingers so they fold inside of the palms. Extend the middle fingers so the tips touch and then interlace the thumbs and index fingers so they form rings around each other, with the fingertips touching. Flip this mudra upside down so the middle fingers are pointed downward at your pelvic region.

Sacral Chakra   Mantra VAM

With your palms in front of your chest, press your pinky and ring fingertips together. Fold your thumbs into your palms, inside of your index and middle finger. You can then press the knuckles of these two fingers together and lower the hands to just below the navel.

Solar Plexus Chakra   Mantra RAM

Place your palms face-up on your thighs. Touch the tips of the thumbs, index fingers, and ring fingers together, straightening through the pinky and middle fingers.

Heart Chakra   Mantra YAM

With your palms at your heart, touch the outer edges of both pinky fingers and thumbs together. Keep the heels of the palms pressed together as you blossom open through your hands. Extend through the tips of all 10 fingers.

Throat Chakra   Mantra HAM

Interlace your last three fingers (middle, ring, and pinky) together inside of your hands. Interlock the index fingertips and thumbs to form two rings, and hold this mudra in front of the base of your throat.

Third Eye Chakra   Mantra AUM

Take your right hand just in front of the space between your eyebrows and curl the ring finger into your palm. Bring the tips of the thumb, middle finger, and index finger to touch, and keep the pinky finger extended long. Place the tips of the three fingers that are touching to your third-eye focal point. The left hand can remain on top of the left thigh, palm face-up, or in Gyan mudra (simply connect the tips of your thumbs with the tips of your index fingers. Relax all your other fingers).

Crown Chakra   Mantra Silence

Place the tips of your index fingers and thumbs together to touch, forming a pyramid shape. Allow the remaining fingers to extend upward, keeping them straight. Raise this mudra to about 6 to 7 inches above the crown of your head.

You can use the mudras or/and mantras after the Chakra Tapping procedure and remember the intention for each chakra. And remember, if you don't have time to go through all the seven chakras you can muscle test which chakra needs the most attention.

Chakra Balancing Tapping Procedure

SOH: Even though some of my chakras may be out of balance, I deeply and completely love, accept and forgive myself. 3x

Or: Even though my ... chakra is out of balance, I deeply and completely love, accept and forgive myself.

Depending on the chakra you could add (example root chakra): Even though I don't feel grounded at this very moment because of all the stress I have, I deeply and completely love, accept and forgive myself.

IE: I feel grounded and safe
OE: I feel centered and stable
UE: I am powerful, rooted, and strong.
N&C: I am financially secure.
CB: The universe will always provide for me.

Tap on your Thymus and take 6 deep breaths

IE: I am in flow with the rhythms of life, inspiration, and creativity.
OE: The sweetness of life flows through me, and I radiate its joy.
UE: I feel safe expressing my sexual self in fun, creative, and healthy ways.
N&C: My emotions are free-flowing and balanced.
CB: I embrace pleasure and abundance.

Tap on your Thymus and take 6 deep breaths

IE: I stand in my personal power.
OE: I make decisions with confidence and conviction.
UE: The only thing I need to control is how I respond to situations.
N&C: I dare to create positive change in my life.
CB: I feel motivated to pursue my purpose.

Tap on your Thymus and take 6 deep breaths

IE: I welcome love with an open heart.
OE: My heart is healed from all the wounds of the past.
UE: I naturally attract love everywhere I go.
N&C: I release and let go of all resentment.
CB: My heart space radiates powerful green light.

Tap on your Thymus and take 6 deep breaths

IE: I communicate confidently and with ease.

OE: I feel comfortable speaking my mind and my inner truth.

UE: I am an active and compassionate listener.

N&C: I express myself with joy and clear intent.

CB: I know when it is time to be still and listen.

Tap on your Thymus and take 6 deep breaths

IE: I trust my intuition.

OE: I feel connected to my spiritual truth.

UE: I let my inner wisdom guide me.

N&C: I trust my decisions.

I quiet my mind with ease.

I am an extension of the universe.

I am infinite and boundless.

I go beyond my limiting beliefs and accept my divine self.

I am divinely guided and inspired.

I am an extension of the universe.

EFT TAPPING WITH BACH FLOWERS

- The Bach Flower Remedy System of healing includes 38 flower essences that were developed by visionary physician, Dr. Edward Bach. Bach had always been more interested in the people suffering disease than in the diseases themselves – a fact that made him unusual at that time.
- The remedies provide powerful support for any type of transition including developmental, seasonal, or any life changes.
- By focusing on and addressing our individual emotional states and personality traits, the Bach Flower Remedies offer a powerful tool for balance and well-being, no matter what you are experiencing.
- Each remedy aids a specific emotion. You can take them individually or mix them to match the way you feel.
- One of the major benefits of the remedies, that is essential while going through any transformational process as well as simply living in our current chaotic times, is the overall balancing and strengthening qualities the remedies offer. The vibrational nature of these essences helps to fortify and nourish our individual energetic system so that we can flow more smoothly through life, stay true to our choices and step forward on our soul path.
- Bach Flower List to test with muscle testing:
  - Agrimony – mental torture behind a cheerful face
  - Aspen – fear of unknown things
  - Beech – intolerance
  - Centaury – the inability to say 'no'
  - Cerato – lack of trust in one's own decisions
  - Cherry Plum – fear of the mind giving way
  - Chestnut Bud – failure to learn from mistakes
  - Chicory – selfish, possessive love
  - Clematis – dreaming of the future without working in the present
  - Crab Apple – the cleansing remedy, also for not liking something about ourselves
  - Elm – overwhelmed by responsibility
  - Gentian – discouragement after a setback
  - Gorse – hopelessness, and despair
  - Heather – talkative self-concern and being self-centered
  - Holly – hatred, envy, and jealousy

- Honeysuckle – living in the past
- Hornbeam – tiredness at the thought of doing something
- Impatiens – impatience
- Larch – lack of confidence
- Mimulus – fear of known things
- Mustard – deep gloom for no reason
- Oak – the plodder who keeps going past the point of exhaustion
- Olive – exhaustion following mental or physical effort
- Pine – guilt
- Red Chestnut – over-concern for the welfare of loved ones
- Rock Rose – terror and fright
- Rock Water – self-denial, rigidity, and self-repression
- Scleranthus – inability to choose between alternatives
- Star of Bethlehem – shock
- Sweet Chestnut – extreme mental anguish, when everything has been tried and there is no light left
- Vervain – over-enthusiasm
- Vine – dominance, and inflexibility
- Walnut – protection from change and unwanted influences
- Water Violet – quiet self-reliance leading to isolation
- White Chestnut – unwanted thoughts and mental arguments
- Wild Oat – uncertainty over one's direction in life
- Wild Rose – drifting, resignation, apathy
- Willow – self-pity, and resentment

For this Tapping Procedure, you may just muscle test the Bach Flowers that you need or tap through all affirmations. Always beginning with the side of your hand, just saying "I deeply and completely love, accept and forgive myself no matter what and I open myself to self-healing and self-growth"

AGRIMONY

I am at peace with myself.
I show others who I really am.
I am honest with myself and others.
I enjoy my own company.
I hold firm when in conflict.

ASPEN
I have all the courage I need.
I open myself to life's experiences.
I have the inner strength to face the future.
I know my world is a safe place.
I am ready for excitement and adventure.

BEECH
I create well-being.
I accept differences in others.
I see everyone's fundamental goodness.
I am gentle and good to myself.

CENTAURY
I meet my own needs.
I am true to myself.
I am in charge of my life.
I stand up for myself.
I value my strength of will.

CERATO
I trust my own thinking.
I know what is right for me.
I trust my own intuition.
I hold myself in high esteem.
I have the courage of my convictions.

CHERRY PLUM
I remain strong under extreme stress.
I am calm and courageous.
I choose to be balanced and stable at all times.
I am as solid as a rock.
I do what is right for me.

CHESTNUT BUD
I learn something new from everything I do.
My past is a source of strength and energy.
I watch and learn from others.

I see things as they really are.
I learn from my mistakes.

CHICORY
I love unconditionally.
I respect the independence of others.
I am worthy of everybody's love.
I have all the attention I need.
I give without thought of return.

CLEMATIS
I am here now.
I am involved in everything I do.
I live every moment well.
I bring my plans to fruition.
My feet are firmly on the ground

CRAB APPLE
I clean myself of unwanted substances.
I deserve to be healthy.
I treat myself with tenderness and care.
I encourage my body to heal itself.
I love myself.

ELM
I have total confidence.
I let go of being a perfectionist.
I am only responsible for the things I choose.
I have the help I need.
I let go of having to do everything.

GENTIAN
I confidently continue to do what is right.
I know each experience is a valuable lesson.
I create my own reality.
I believe in ultimate success.
I am determined to persevere.

GORSE
I have faith in life itself.
I decide to be optimistic.
I believe in myself.
I have hope and confidence in the future.
I look on the bright side.

HEATHER
I take care of all my own needs.
I am a willing listener.
I am always ready to help out.
I love spending time on my own.
I let go of being needy.

HOLLY
I am at one with the world.
I open my heart to others.
I radiate love, joy, and happiness.
I love to see others succeed.
I deserve the love of others.

HONEYSUCKLE
I let go of old memories that hold me back.
I come from my past and move to my future.
I live in the present.
I plunge into life.
I welcome the future.

HORNBEAM
I have the energy I need.
I am strong and fulfilled.
I live my life effortlessly.
I am awake and fresh.
I get my life how I want it.

IMPATIENS
I have patience and understanding.
I have all the time I need.

I take the time to appreciate others.
I live my life calmly and gently.
I take things slowly when I choose.

LARCH
I act with total confidence.
I always expect to succeed.
I am excited by every new challenge.
I act with boldness and determination.
I express myself creatively.

MIMULUS
I act with courage and inner strength.
I recognize each difficulty as an opportunity.
I meet each challenge with my sense of humor.
The world is my oyster.
I can do anything.

MUSTARD
I am the source of light and strength.
I have serenity and peace of mind.
My heart sings.
I reclaim my radiance and joy.

OAK
I am strong and energetic.
I always give myself a break when I need it.
I rest deeply.
I am open and spontaneous.
I let go of struggling so hard.

OLIVE
I use my energy in the best possible way.
I recognize my own needs.
I restore my own vitality and strength.
I know my priorities in giving to others.

PINE

I let go of guilt and self-blame.
I take responsibility for all that I do.
I forgive myself for blaming myself.
I always did the best I could.
I am already completely good enough.
I accept and approve of myself.

RED CHESTNUT

I radiate peace and calm.
I protect myself from the problems of others.
I maintain my psychic space.
I expect positive outcomes.
I send calm loving thoughts to those in need.

ROCK ROSE

My spirit lives.
I'm ready for anything.
I have courage in a crisis.
I am in touch with my inherent power.

ROCK WATER

I flow with my own natural rhythm.
I always stay relaxed.
I am adaptable and flexible.
I look after myself well.
I enjoy the pleasures of life.

SCLERANTHUS

I know what is right for me.
I think clearly and decide easily.
I act on my decisions confidently.
I am clear and consistent.
I always find elegant solutions.

STAR OF BETHLEHEM

I recovered from past trauma.
I am calm, and my soul is soothed.

I have inner peace.
My energy flows smoothly.

SWEET CHESTNUT

I trust in life itself.
I ask for all the help I need.
I come out of the darkness and into the light.
I open myself to changing and growing.

VERVAIN

I believe in the strength of my example.
I respect the rights of others.
I trust myself as I trust others.
I encourage others to become strong and powerful.
I am sensitive and compassionate.
I am in touch with my inner self.

VINE

I believe in the strength of my example
I respect the rights of others
I trust myself as I trust others
I encourage others to become strong and powerful
I am sensitive and compassionate
I am in touch with my inner self

WALNUT

I free myself from all negative influences.
I follow my inner guidance.
I'm ready for a change.
I break through to fulfill my potential.
I am blossoming.

WATER VIOLET

I enjoy being with others.
I open myself to giving and receiving.
I can have warm close loving relationships.
I share my thoughts, my visions, and my dreams.
I express my love for others.

WHITE CHESTNUT

I am calm and serene.

I bring myself to calmness and tranquility.

From my quiet mind, answers emerge.

I am at peace with myself.

I develop my intuition.

WILD OAT

I create the opportunities I need.

I have a strong sense of purpose.

I have definite ambitions to fulfill.

I follow my life direction.

WILD ROSE

I am alive with an interest in life.

I have enthusiasm for everything I do.

I sparkle with vitality.

I have the spirit and joy of adventure.

WILLOW

I forgive others as I forgive myself.

I let go of blame and bitterness.

I see things from their true perspective.

I take responsibility for my relationships.

I see the best in others.

I give my unconditional love and support.

RESCUE REMEDY: Clematis, Cherry Plum, Impatiens, Rock Rose, & Star of Bethlehem

EFT TAPPING WITH THE SEDONA METHOD

The Sedona Method was developed by Lester Levenson after he was given three months to live. He then lived another 42 years. Lester was a man who loved challenges. Instead of giving up, he decided to go back to the lab within himself and find some answers. Because of his determination and concentration, he was able to cut through his conscious mind to find what is needed. What he found was the ultimate tool for personal growth - a way of letting go of all inner limitations. He was so excited by his discovery that he used it intensively for three months. By the end of that period, he entered a state of profound peace that never left him, and his body became completely healthy again.

The Sedona Method identifies the root emotions as the central cause of suffering. It is the experience of the method's founder, Lester Levenson, that all or nearly all of the main suffering emotions **AGFLAP - Apathy, Grief, Fear, Lust, Anger, Pride** have behind them a need for approval, control, and security/ survival/ safety.

In this method, the non-suffering feelings are **CAP - Courageousness, Acceptance, and Peace**.

The ultimate goal is **imperturbability (empty, silent, and at peace)**.

The basic method can be summed up as:

1) become aware of the feeling,
2) feel (acknowledge that you have this emotion) the feeling,
3) identify the feeling (allow it, show self-compassion, tapping at the side of the hand),
4) relax into the feeling, (tap through the EFT Tapping procedure)
5) until you feel the release (number on the scale going down to zero)

Begin by allowing yourself to notice where your problem is not. Even your worst problem is not always with you in the present moment NOW. Start to become aware of your basic nature of unbounded freedom: Stop the habit of looking for your problems when they are not there.

Easily allow yourself to become aware of your SENSORY PERCEPTIONS, (AUDITORY, VISUALLY, THINKING, KINESTHETIC SENSATIONS).

Could you allow yourself just to have the perception of whatever it is in this very moment? And then, could you allow yourself to also notice and welcome the silence, emptiness, and space that surrounds and interpenetrates whatever it is you perceive? And switch back and forth between the two perceptions playfully?

The AGFLAP-CAP chart tells us that the emotional states of courageousness and acceptance are both loving. Acceptance includes the following synonyms: friendly, gracious, embracing, considerate, compassionate, and understanding. To walk in love towards ourselves and towards others, we need to have the kind of qualities seen in courageousness, such as awareness, cheerfulness, compassion, competence, confidence, decisiveness, enthusiasm, flexibility, giving, loving, self-sufficiency, and supportiveness.

Now, let's have a look at a PARTICULAR PROBLEM, and welcome that memory with all the pictures, sounds, sensations, thoughts, and feelings that are associated with it? Could you allow yourself to notice how most of your experience happens through your sensory perceptions and apart from the actual problem? And, could you allow yourself to welcome at least the possibility that this problem is not as all-consuming as it has seemed?

The SEDONA METHOD Release Process combined with EFT Tapping:

1. Tap on the side of the hand: Although I see, hear, think, feel … (sensory perception) about the memory/problem … I deeply and completely love accept and forgive myself. (3x with a different perception)
2. Muscle Test:
   Could I allow this feeling to be here?
   Could I welcome this feeling?
   Could I let this feeling go?
   Am I willing to let it go?
   (Just notice the answers without judgment)
3. Would I rather have this feeling? (subconscious saboteur → the feeling keeps you SAFE)
4. Would I rather be free? (Yes! → Celebrate)
5. If there is resistance, tap through the whole tapping sequence and say, "I choose to let go of the resistance now."
6. Draw an infinity eight with your finger. Follow with your eyes (without moving your head) and say, "I'm ready to let go of the resistance and I choose to be free!"

7. Allow your attention to drop into your heart. Take six breaths rewire your brain and make the process last.

Of course, there's more to this technique, but this book is about inspiring you to playfully experiment with different tools that can all be combined with EFT.

CHAPTER FOUR

EMOTIONAL RELEASE THROUGH EXPRESSIVE ARTS THERAPY WORKBOOK

- Expressive Art Therapy – Language Of Symbols & Metaphors
- The ART Of Tapping – A marriage of Expressive Arts Therapy & EFT Tapping
- Emotional Release Exercises
- Body Mapping & Narrative Therapy
- Ideograms & Metaphors
- NLP Timeline
- Emotional Empowerment Exercises
- The Tree Metaphor
- Dance and Movement Therapy
- Walking Meditation & Chakra Dancing

EXPRESSIVE ART THERAPY – THE LANGUAGE OF SYMBOLS AND METAPHORS

Language is originally and essentially nothing but a system of signs or symbols, which denote real occurrences, or their echo in the human soul. Symbolic or nonlinear thinking is holistic, right-brain oriented; it is complementary to logical, linear, left-brain thinking.

Chinese proverb: "One picture is worth ten thousand words."

The development of deep metaphors begins at birth, and they continue being shaped with our social environment. In this sense, metaphors are involved with language, emotion, and our innate abilities. Metaphors work unconsciously. They are essential ways in our language of defining ideas. Our conceptual system, the very way that we perceive our world, is fundamentally metaphorical in nature.

Metaphors analyze two objects and collate them by suggesting that two objects are similar to each other, as well as they are quite unlike. Metaphors allow obtaining information from a fresh point of view and thus improve new learning methods. Visual metaphors are a concept that demonstrates how visual imagination is systematized by meanings through culture and experiences. Forms, icons, and symbols may represent different meanings and show up in different appearances as visual metaphors, but they express the same influence across cultures. We create metaphors to understand the concepts that are based on our experiences and actions. A sound, sometimes a picture or a word may represent feelings and ideas, and how we perceive a concept metaphorically. Metaphors are usually based on emotions, even when verbal or visual.

Metaphors speak to the heart and it is only with the heart that one can see rightly*. For this reason, metaphors have long been the language of mystics, spiritual teachers, poets, storytellers, and other expressive artists. A Metaphor is a "heart tool" that helps us explore the ideas, forces, and powers that lie behind our rational thought.

*In Antoine de Saint-Exupery's book *The Little Prince* we learn a simple secret from the fox: ***"And now here is my secret, a very simple secret: It is only with the heart that one can see rightly; what is essential is invisible to the eye."***

Many psychologists and therapists have affirmed the value of using metaphors to:

- **Find patterns that aren't working**
- **Motivate clients in a positive direction**
- **Help clients cope with life's obstacles**
- **Improve mental health by seeing the big picture**
- **Communicate to others about one's thoughts**

Metaphors do this by providing figurative meaning and comparison that help make sense of abstract and complicated concepts.

THE POWER OF EXPRESSIVE ARTS THERAPY

Art Therapy in general combines visual art and psychotherapy in a creative process using the created image as a foundation for self-exploration and understanding. Thoughts and feelings often reach expression in images rather than words. Through the use of art therapy, feelings and inner conflicts can be projected into visual form. In the creative act, conflict is re-experienced, resolved, and integrated. - The B.C. Art Therapy Association

Art therapy improves self-awareness and self-esteem. Art therapy is very beneficial for people struggling with:

- **Life transitions**
- **Relationship issues – Divorce – Separation – Co-dependency, etc.**
- **Addictions**
- **Depression – Anxiety – Post Traumatic Stress Disorder – Grief & Loss**
- **Anxiety – Phobias – Eating Disorders**

The Marriage of EFT And Expressive Art Therapy Gives Birth To "The Art Of Tapping"

Developed by Monika Marguerite Lux during counseling sessions with teens in transition suffering from social phobias, different anxieties, traumatic childhood and first loss & grief experiences, teen depression or PTSD.

"Sometimes we live our lives like puzzle pieces turned upside down - only showing the world our gray sides. Then along comes life, and it starts flipping them over, showing to us and the world more than just the outline of who we are - it shows us the colors. If we can start to turn more over and put them together, we can see the picture of who we really emerge."
~Manifest~

While many of us may find it hard to put our feelings about a tough experience from the past into words, drawing a picture or piecing together a collage can help us convey our sadness, regret, or anger clearly, giving us the much-needed chance to release those negative emotions. Many counselors find art therapy just as effective (and sometimes even more so) as other practices that help us uncover different aspects of our personalities and cope with challenges or traumas.

Later on, in my practice, I used The Art Of Tapping with seniors. It helped one of my clients to heal a miscarriage she had over 50 years ago. She had suffered from a deep "unknown" sadness ever since not aware that it was linked to a traumatic experience that long ago. She painted a beautiful picture with a rose for her daughter, named her Barbara, and integrated her soul into her family system.

Another senior client booked a session because she felt overwhelmed by life circumstances and was looking for a way to put all her life's "puzzle pieces" together to see and UNDERSTAND the whole picture. Through art and tapping finally, everything made sense to her and filled her deeply with gratitude for all her accomplishments in her truly meaningful life.

EMOTIONAL RELEASE EXERCISES

Journaling & Drawing – The Puzzle Of Life

Take a journal or piece of paper and write a story about a chapter in your life that still "puzzles" you.

Start tapping on the side of your hand:

Even though I still don't understand… I deeply and completely love, accept and forgive myself. Maybe it's not necessary to understand but trust my inner healer to show me the way.

Write down whatever surfaces: emotions, thoughts, beliefs

Draw a picture or symbol for this chapter in your life. Your subconscious will understand what it is all about.

Tap on the side of your hand:

Even though there is this circle, square… / even though it has this … color, shape and I don't know what it means, I deeply and completely love, accept and forgive myself.

Even though there is this emotion of… surfacing now, I deeply and completely love, accept and forgive myself.

Tap on the top of your head and your heart:

I choose to let it go!

Switch hands:

It's safe to let it go!

Tap your wrists/pulse points together.

Assume the heart-healing position:

I'm at peace!

Take 6 deep healing breaths and imagine how you release this chapter of your past through your feet into the EARTH.

Non-Dominant Hand Drawing – Conversation With Your Higher Self

Drawing with your non-dominant hand allows you to silence your inner critic.

When you write with your dominant hand (regardless of whether you are left- or right-handed), you access the logical, linear, verbal part of your mind. This is the everyday mind, and it dominates our culture.

Switching hands activates what we think of as the right brain – the creative, holistic, subconscious, intuitive brain – that tends to be underdeveloped and underutilized.

The right brain is not concerned with protecting our ego and preserving the status quo. It's more about reflecting the truth as we understand it. The subconscious is constantly absorbing and processing information, sending up hunches, flashes of insight, gut feelings. By switching the pen to your non-dominant hand, it's like you find a way to surface this hidden stream of nonverbal intelligence and translate it to words on the page.

Set your intention to work on a specific issue or traumatic event in your life. Let the most important aspect about it be downloaded from your subconscious mind and sent through your arm, to your hand, to the pen, and onto the paper in front of you into a spontaneous movement, drawing, scribble, or doodling. ***Your pen is NOT supposed to leave the paper. The movement is fast and short.***

Leave your hand on the scribble, gaze at it with soft eyes. Ask your subconscious mind to bring up a memory from the past related to your spontaneous scribble and write it down with all the details you can remember. Look at the core emotions. Write down how you felt (for example abandoned, not heard, rejected, etc.)

Close your eyes and imagine your younger self, just after the traumatic event. Acknowledge your emotions. You had every right to feel them. Take the hands of this beautiful child, that had to endure so much pain and with a firm voice tell it: "I am very sorry for leaving you alone. I acknowledge your suffering. You had the right to feel the way you felt after this incident. Please forgive me as I forgive myself. I love you deeply and I accept myself completely for who I am. Thank you for helping me release and gaining back my power." Repeat while tapping on the side of your hand and top of the head & heart points. Release while breathing deeply and assuming the Heart Healing Posture.

Two-Hand Drawings – Live Chat

Have two pieces of paper in front of you. Attach them to the table with some adhesive tape. You may put on some music that inspires you. Now, you can do two different exercises and then tap on whatever comes up.

Take a pencil in each hand and draw some abstract lines and shapes with both of your hands at the same time. Abstract drawing means drawing with artistic inspiration but without specific intentions in mind. Let your hands be moved totally by the creative spirit.

Reflect on how this feels to you.

- **How are your hands communicating with each other?**
- **What is the communication about?**
- **Did you have a certain issue in mind or did a certain issue come up while you were drawing?**
- **Are your hands circling in the same or opposite direction?**
- **Are they playing together as a team or are there some difficulties within the communication?**
- **How does this activity make you feel?**
- **What emotions can you sense?**
- **What does "flow" mean to you?**
- **Is the movement or "flow" of one or both hands interrupted?**
- **Does one hand move faster than the other?**

Write the answers in your journal and start tapping through the sequence. Example: "Even though my left hand moved faster than my right hand, I deeply and completely love, accept and forgive myself. I acknowledge that at this moment one hand moves faster than the other. It might be different tomorrow and I don't have to know why. I trust my higher self to guide me to heal myself and find happiness."

Again, take your pencils. Just this time, you ask a question with your right hand on any issue that's bothering you and answer with your left hand. Remember, it's about abstract drawing. Questions and Answers will appear in front of you as patterns, lines, and shapes.

You are going to tap on the answer. Example: "Even though I look at the lines and might not understand consciously, my higher self knows how to decipher the subconscious code and I trust the process. I deeply and completely love, accept and forgive myself. I acknowledge and honor the answer and all the emotions that come with it. It's time to move on. It's time to re-create. It's time to let go of what no longer serves me."

Bilateral Guided Drawing

Bilateral guided drawing is a mindfulness exercise that is used to support body mapping (next chapter) in a trauma-informed way and to integrate the left and right brain functions, required to work in unison to help create an inner acceptance or awareness and to trust intuition and life force.

Bilateral guided drawing is a powerful approach that helps to uncover frozen or forgotten memories from within the body and does not promote the need for the client to push through any memories. It allows the client to take their time in recognizing the emotional distress caused by an event from their past and enables them to move through the event slowly and with ease, one aspect of the event at a time.

Choose a relaxing or rhythmic (tribal) piece of music for your drawing. You can use a poster-size paper or just stick two small sheets together, to have enough space for both of your hands to draw at the same time.

Think of any traumatic event you would like to heal and let go of for good. Remember, loss equals trauma and loss can be anything from not being promoted to having to move to another place.

Trust your intuition and decide if you feel like drawing a particular emotion, thought, dialogue, conflict, shape, color, lines, or rhythm.

Remember, there are always two sides to everything in life. Maybe your bilateral drawing shows you the cons and pros of an event. Perhaps one picture shows the light and one the shadow.

Or one picture shows you where you are right now and the one next to it shows you the way to move on.

There are limitless possibilities for how to read your artwork. Again, trust your gut-heart intuition.

I often find rhythmic drawing the most healing approach to release even deep-seated trauma because you move your whole body.

You may reflect on one of the following questions:

- **How does this resonate in your body?**
- **Do you know this sensation? Is it familiar?**
- **Have you felt it before? When?**
- **Are you ready to let it go during the process? How do you have to move to let it go?**

As it is important to engage through movements that go beyond the use of the hands to involve the whole body in natural rhythms you can start with large swinging gestures that come from the shoulder, elbow, or wrist to not only liberate creative expression but also act in a restorative capacity to support healthy rhythms in your body and mind.

In other words, you can practice these rhythmic movements in the air first and then later transfer them to paper with drawing materials.

Alternate Hands on the same drawing

Another possibility is to draw lines or shapes with one hand and then, while tracing them with the other hand, become aware of what's happening inside of you regarding feelings, emotions, thoughts, tension, pain, etc.

BODY MAPPING

Let us tap into the wisdom of the body by activating levels of body consciousness through creative exploration, body centering activities, and meditation.

It's a process where we are in a place of deep listening and inner connection with the stories of the body we have created through lived experience.

Working with a life-size canvas of ourselves allows for self-reflection and deep resonance. Body Mapping creates an exchange between our inner wisdom and outer creativity through creative play. The deep listening and inner awareness create an intimate bonding and relationship with who we really are, our true selves. This allows us to hear and acknowledge our stories, heal them through our vast inner wisdom, let them go as they don't feel up to date anymore, and recreate a new purpose and meaningful life.

During this "artful" and creative process, we may notice what has transformed, or we may acknowledge what needs to be explored further or let go of. Either way, there is something powerful, and often compassionate that unfolds naturally.

Essentially body mapping helps us reconnect to our embodied self.

If you don't have a poster-size canvas or packing paper roll. Just use the following diagrams below.

1. **Tune In To Your Body.**
    Sit in a quiet place where you are undisturbed. Relax your body and begin to sense the sensations in your body. You can do PATH, noticing Pressure, Air, Tension, and Heat, if you like, to tune in.

2. **Tension.**
    Pay attention to any areas where you feel TENSION and how it's represented.

3. **Draw & Color.**
    Fill in the TENSION on your Body Mapping Diagram, either using a pen for marking or paint/crayons for coloring.

4. **Deepen Attention For 6 Deep Breaths.**

   Rest your attention on just ONE area that you feel TENSION. Keep your attention resting on that spot without moving it away for 6 breaths. If you feel the temptation to wander off, remind yourself to come back to the special area of focus.

5. **Bring to Mind an Oasis Spot.**

   An oasis spot is a location – inside the body, in the imagination, or in nature – where there is complete calm and peace. It embodies the "calm and alert (energetic)" state that is natural to all living beings when they are feeling safe.

   Examples:

   1. A place within the body that feels unperturbed, natural, still, serene, and calm (this may change from day to day, so be alert to the true sensation at the present and if there are body parts outside your awareness, activated, tense or holding nervous or stuck energy)
   2. A place in nature that you feel calmness emanating from, like water running down a creek, soft blades of grass in the lawn, moss in a forest, pine trees, a flower patch, branches of a tree, clouds. This can even be a memory of a place you have experienced.
   3. An animal or a pet like a sleeping cat or a spirit (wild) animal
   4. A place within the imagination like a cave within your heart, or a huge shell, or a place at the beach that you found in a guided meditation

   In this exercise, we will tune into an Oasis Spot in nature. Think about a place in nature familiar to you, or within your field of vision (like clouds out the window). Bring it to mind and close your eyes.

6. **Focus on Space.**

   Now pay attention to the space in and around this Oasis Spot. Try to sense the space between the blades of grass, the space between clouds, between branches or trees. Rest your attention on this space for 6 breaths. You might wonder, what would it feel like to be that space?

7. **Pendulation.**

   Rest your awareness back on your body and sense a place of TENSION (the same or a different one). Rest your awareness there for 6 breaths. Then rest your awareness on the Oasis Spot you have in mind. Rest there for 6 breaths. Keep going back and forth. Go back and forth until you feel a shift in the overall felt sense in your body.

8. **Draw & Color.**
   If you use two shapes to compare before and after, go to the second paper and color or draw in the areas that feel different now, you can use your imagination and draw any symbols and colors you like.

9. **Repeat the above steps, this time for FEAR.**
   You may use the same diagrams or print out two additional diagrams.

10. **You may do the other emotions that you feel drawn to:**
    Absent Numb Nothing (Repressed Frozen), Angry, Sorrow, Regret, Guilt, etc. Two emotions are usually enough for one sitting but use your own judgment. You may do them all at one time if you feel strong enough.

You are now finished. Congratulations on taking care of yourself and your healing!

Body Map Story Telling

Different Parts:

- **Testimony or Narrative:** What's the story you tell yourself about your life?
- **Self-Portrait & Body Posture:** We all have the same features placed in more or less the same way on our faces, yet we all look different, and our faces mean different things to different people. How would you like to represent your face and your body posture? As it appears? or in a more symbolic way? What do you want to express or communicate with your body posture?
- **Colors:** How do you want colors to represent certain parts, emotions, pain, etc. in your body?
- **New Life Journey:** Take a few minutes to look at your body map and think about what it says. In a few words tell your story about your journey through your body map and how you would like to be remembered by others.
- **Marks On and Under the skin:** I would like you to think about how to represent your life conditions, your relationship with others, and how these things impact your body and your well-being. What kind of figures, symbols or images represent your life right now? Now, if you look from head to toe on your body map, can you identify any specific marks on your body that are related to past trauma or current health? How did you get these marks on your body? What happened? On a day-to-day basis, what do you do to heal and release your burden for good?

- **Personal Symbol (of strength) and (Power) Slogan:** What personal symbol and slogan have you chosen to describe your traumatic experience? Who are you as a person? What is your life philosophy? What keeps you going? Can you explain the meaning of your symbol and slogan? Where on your body map would you like to place these symbols and why?

- **Body Scan and Personal Values:** Now, I want you to explore all aspects of your social life. This includes issues related to gender, race, and friendship(s). Have you ever faced challenges in your social, spiritual, emotional life? What kind of difficulties or challenges were these? (e.g. gender-based discrimination, racism, exclusion from services, etc.) Now I want you to think about your strength and courage when facing these problems. Where does your strength come from? Where do you get the courage to keep moving forward? Scan your body map and focus on finding where this personal strength comes from. You might also want to look at your values and check how they may collide with some people and harmonize with others. Do your courage and motivations come from your arms? Your mind? Is it related to your personal slogan?

- **Support Structure:** I would like you to identify key people, groups, or things in your life that support you or help you cope with some of the challenges you face. Who gives you support? It can be an organization, a person, your spirituality. How do these people show their support? What does this support mean to you and where is it in or around your body?

- **Future:** I would like you to think about your future. How do you imagine your future? What is your vision, your goal, or your dream (It may be something material, physical, emotional, or spiritual)? What are you working towards? What do you think will happen? Where do you think you will be?

- **Message to Others:** What message would you like to give to the public about your life experience? Why is it important for the public to know this? Where on the body map do you want to put your message?

Body Front View

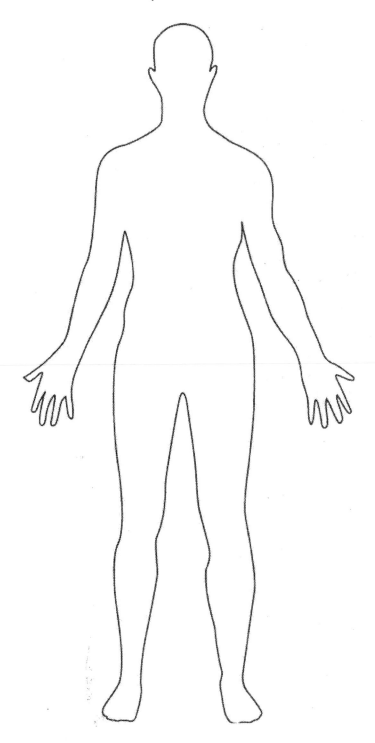

Body Back View

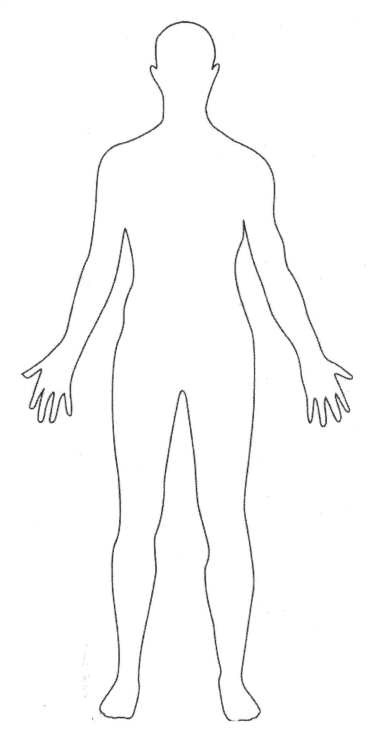

IDEOGRAMS & METAPHORS – HEALING SYMBOLS FROM THE SACRED PLACE OF YOUR HEART

"The soul never thinks without an image." ~ Aristotle

UNIVERSAL SHAPES have significant psychological and mythological meanings embedded in our minds. Life is art and stories have shapes that support our very own processes of growth. The language of the unconscious and the deep inner self is comprised of imagery (shapes), metaphors, and feelings.

We construct our world through **METAPHOR**. We can only conceptualize by making comparisons between different realms of experience.

A metaphor shows us one thing as another, and in doing so extends the way we see the world, also often refreshing and enlivening our perception. In oral and written language, using the medium of picture imagery, metaphor speaks directly to our imaginative faculties, bypassing our rational brain. Such metaphoric byways and pathways enable us to explore the ideas, forces, and powers that lie behind or beyond our rational thought and help us in overcoming the limitations of our fixed categories.

IDEOGRAMS are the written physical language between you and your subconscious mind. Each ideogram is a symbol for an idea, a concept, or a thing. We refer to the ideas, concepts, and things that ideograms represent as gestalts.

Again, with your non-dominant hand, fill part or all of the page, moving more rapidly until you reach the point of letting go of control and surrender to the actual message of your subconscious, creating a picture of shapes melting into each other until the movement comes to an end. Stay with this stillness and emptiness, gazing at the picture in front of you. Put the pen aside and start tapping on whatever comes up.

For example: "Even though there is this circle, and it feels uncomfortable, threatening, unknown…, I deeply and completely love, accept and forgive myself." "This line, it feels abrasive. This triangle pokes into my heart. When I look at the picture, anger surfaces. etc."

It doesn't have to make sense to your left brain. The Art Of Tapping is a right-brain process. You tap along with all your sensual perceptions: visual, auditory, kinesthetic, olfactory, gustatory. If there were colors, what would you see? If there were sounds, what would you hear?

You may take some watercolors, colored pencils, or crayons and color your scribble (nowadays, that's called "Zentangle"). What does it look like when it's colored? What colors did you use? Do they make you feel good?

Perhaps there was a shift happening while you were painting and coloring. Something may have changed from feeling uncomfortable to being at peace, looking at your unique piece of art. Summon the release and courage to surrender the old and emerge like the Phoenix from the ashes of your past.

This is a spontaneously drawn scribble Rule: Trust the reactions of your body without exception. Your body always tells the truth. Trust it. And always trust the very first reaction. Never anticipate what your Universal Ideogram should look like, just let your body give you the shape, as quickly as possible.

The ideogram is an amazing phenomenon. It holds the taste, color, temperature, emotions, activity - everything there is to know about your issue, traumatic event, anxiety, etc. in a very small package.

You may also try to tap the EFT points with your right hand while moving the pen with your left hand or vice versa.

NLP TIMELINE – MAKE YOUR VISIONS COME TRUE

NLP TIMELINES are a technique where the practitioner utilizes a client's metaphors of time, to allow the unconscious mind to access 'past' representations and to move on from 'stuck patterns' that have a history. Let's eliminate some obstacles and challenges, by traveling along the timeline and using EFT Tapping to get unstuck and reach whatever goal we set. This is a powerful process! It often gives people a sense of freedom, relief, and closure. As practitioners, we are looking at the structure of the historic representation, not the content, always keeping in mind that memories can change over time and maybe heavily distorted and deleted.

Using the NLP Timeline Technique allows us to take the benefit of our wisdom and experience as adults back to our younger selves. We give them the gift of the insight, strength, or perspective we would have liked in that moment or over those childhood years. We are RE-PARENTING our INNER CHILD – filling in the gaps, healing the timeline up to the present day, and integrating the soul part that has been struggling for so long.

"Until you make the unconscious conscious, it will direct your life and you will call it fate." – **C. G. Jung**

Just as we can take positive resources back into the past to support our younger selves, we can project them forward to help our future selves. We can identify what it is that we really desire, how we want to live and what resources we need to make our vision a reality. Then, to manifest it, we need to experience ourselves living life that way using all our senses. It's like stepping into the shoes of your future self and noticing all the details that really matter to you.

"I am not what happened to me, I am what I choose to become." - **C. G. Jung**

Draw three pictures:

1st picture	2nd picture	3rd picture
Past	Presence	Future
Traumatic/negative (childhood) experience	How does your past affect your NOW?	Goals, Visions & Dreams

Put the pictures on the floor as far away from each other as the size of the room allows. Imagine there is an invisible path between them (you can also put a rope between them or draw a line).

You can step into each of the energy fields, become aware of their messages, and jot them down in your journal.

Or you can step into today's picture, close your eyes and check in with yourself what direction your body is drawn to face. Often some issues in the past have to be resolved to access all the resources we need to create the future of our dreams. Sometimes when you stand in the present field looking towards the future you feel pulled back or totally stuck in place, unable to move at all.

Then step into the future picture and look back. Is there anything else that needs healing?

In each energy field, become aware of your posture.

- Is there any tension in your body?
- Are you standing taller and more up straight in one of the fields?
- Are your hands open or closed tight in fists?
- Are you tempted to fold your arms tightly across your chest in one of the fields, while you feel open and relaxed in the other one?
- What about your other senses?
- Are there different sounds or smells within the fields?

Put a paper next to each field and write down what's different.

To start the process, step into your past and slowly move along the timeline until you feel an invisible barrier.

If you have no clue what it is about, muscle test your age and who was involved in the traumatic memory. Tap on the side of your hand and say "It's ok for the memory to come up. I deeply and completely love, accept and forgive myself."

As soon as you can remember the event, keep acknowledging that it happened, allow each emotion to surface, and welcome it with unconditional love, knowing you did the best you could with the tools you had back then.

Ask your inner child what it needs from you to heal. Ask your inner child if you can tap on them or surrogate tap on all the traumatic aspects that keep coming up until you feel inner peace. Then ask if you can release the trapped emotion or trauma for good.

Send HEALING into the presence.

Step into the NOW.

What has changed? Do you have access to resources you weren't even aware of before?

Slowly start moving towards your future.

Do you feel stuck again at any point along the way? Is something still slowing you down? Does something surface you haven't been aware of before?

Go back to where it started, resolve, heal and release for good.

You can also go to a moment in your past before the traumatic event even happened and see what created it.

Be curious and playful! Explore different positions and discover the lessons you can learn and the insights you can gain.

Questions to ask and time periods to look at:

- When was the first time I had this special emotion, stopping me from moving forward and reaching my goal?
- Inherited through generations (family history)? Before birth, during conception? During pregnancy (in the womb) During birth?

Age 0-7	**- the 'imprint' period (Up to the age of seven, we are like sponges, absorbing everything around us and accepting much of it as true, especially when it comes from our parents. The confusion and blind belief of this period can also lead to the early formation of trauma and other deep problems.).**
Age 7–14	**- the 'modeling period' (we tend to have 'heroes' and role models).**
Age 14–21	**- the 'socializing period' (we begin establishing relationships)**

- At age 0-5, 5-10, etc.? Trust your subconscious mind and accept the first thing that comes up (this is usually the accurate one).
- Who was involved? Parents? Siblings? Relatives? Partners?
- Can I release it now?

Start tapping on the side of your hand. "Even though there was … (this incident), I deeply and completely love, accept and forgive myself. And I choose to release NOW all that no longer serves me in a positive and productive way."

Tap through the sequence "I acknowledge this emotion. It was alright to feel it then. But now I don't have to hold on to it anymore. I choose to release it/it's time to release it now/I'm ready to release it now etc."

Hold your ESR points.

Place your hands in a heart-healing position and take 6 deep breaths.

Self-muscle test if the stuckness/block is gone.

EMOTIONAL EMPOWERMENT EXERCISES

The theory behind tapping is that negative emotions disrupt the flow of energy through the meridians, creating disharmony and imbalances in the body. The spoken statements keep your mind focused on the incident and its difficult memories while the tapping releases the associated blocked energy. The combination of tapping on specific points along with verbal statements gently realigns the body's energy system and natural flow. I found that each emotional release creates a bit of a void that needs to be filled with a sense of safety, love, and personal empowerment.

Your Safe Place

Think about a place where you would feel absolutely safe and loved. What would it look like? It can be a place in nature (lake, river, ocean, forest, mountain, meadow, etc.), a fantasy place ("Sacred Bubble", "Magic Shell" etc.), a room in a house that only exists in your dreams... Choose your favorite art technique (watercolors, crayons, markers, pencils, etc.) and draw or paint this safe place. It's YOUR place! It's always with you in your heart. You can always return to it, to recover, recharge and revive. And you can put your painting on the floor to step into the energy field of "SAFETY, LOVE, and PROTECTION". Close your eyes and fill the void.

Ask yourself: What color, what smell, what sound, what taste, what feeling suggests stability and safety?

Tap through the sequence, looking at your finished picture:

Side Of The Hand: Even though I sometimes feel scared and alone, I deeply and completely love, accept and forgive myself. But there's a place, a place of safety, a place filled with unconditional love... There's this beautiful color. I can smell. I hear. I taste. When I touch (water, grass, walls, etc.) it feels (warm, smooth, like silk, etc.) This place will be in my heart forever and I can return at any given time and relax for a while... recharge my batteries... focusing on my breath. Breathe in and say/think "slow down", breathe out and say/think "relax".

"Breathing in, I calm body and mind. Breathing out, I smile. Dwelling in the present moment I know this is the only moment." ~ Thich Nhat Hanh

Unconditional Love

What does unconditional love look like?   Paint your picture or write about it in your journal
When did you feel unconditionally loved?   (For me, I first felt this kind of Love when I received
the first Reiki treatment from my Reiki master.)
How did it feel?   (For me, it was a feeling of belonging and oneness)

How were your 5 senses involved in the experience?

Tap through the EFT sequence with everything you see in your picture (those flowing lines, the fusion of colors, the round shape, etc. like we did it before).

If a positive memory pops up in your mind include it in the tapping.

Think gratitude! Give thanks to the unique friend or family member who loves and accepts you just the way you are, or like I did to CREATION/THE UNIVERSE.

Say a prayer, like HO'OPONOPONO.

Tap to "When I started loving myself" - A poem by Charlie Chaplin written on his 70th birthday on April 16, 1959

IE: As I began to love myself, I found that anguish and emotional suffering are only warning signs that I was living against my own truth. Today, I know, this is **"AUTHENTICITY"**.

OE: As I began to love myself, I understood how much it can offend somebody
As I try to force my desires on this person, even though I knew the time was not right and the person was not ready for it, and even though this person was me. Today I call it **"RESPECT"**.

UE: As I began to love myself, I stopped craving for a different life, and I could see that everything that surrounded me was inviting me to grow. Today I call it **"MATURITY"**.

N&C: As I began to love myself, I understood that under any circumstance, I am in the right place at the right time, and everything happens at the exact right moment. So, I could be calm. Today I call it **"SELF-CONFIDENCE"**.

C&N: As I began to love myself, I quit steeling my own time, and I stopped designing huge projects for the future. Today, I only do what brings me joy and happiness, things I love to do and that make my heart cheer, and I do them in my own way and in my own rhythm. Today I call it **"SIMPLICITY"**.

KP: As I began to love myself, I freed myself of anything that is no good for my health – food, people, things, situations, and everything that drew me down and away from myself. At first, I called this attitude a healthy egoism. Today I know it is **"LOVE OF ONESELF"**.

LP: As I began to love myself, I quit trying to always be right, and ever since I was wrong less of the time. Today I discovered that is **"MODESTY"**.

UA: As I began to love myself. I refused to go on living in the past and worry about the future. Now, I only live for the moment, where EVERYTHING is happening. Today I live each day, day by day, and I call it **"FULFILLMENT"**.

3rd E: As I began to love myself, I recognized that my mind can disturb me and it can make me sick. But As I connected it to my heart, my mind became a valuable ally. Today I call this connection **"WISDOM OF THE HEART"**.

H&H: We no longer need to fear arguments, confrontations, or any kind of problems with ourselves or others. Even stars collide, and out of their crashing new worlds are born. Today I know **THAT IS "LIFE"**!

End with placing your hands in a heart-healing position and take 6 deep breaths.

"How you love yourself is how you teach others to love you."—*Rupi Kaur, Milk, and Honey.*

"I now see how owning our story and loving ourselves through that process is the bravest thing that we will ever do."—*Brené Brown*

"Document the moments you feel most in love with yourself—what you're wearing, who you're around, what you're doing. Recreate and repeat."—*Warsan Shire*

"To find a happy ending with someone else, first you have to find it alone."—*Soman Chainani*

"Respect yourself and others will respect you."—*Confucius*

YOUR Personal Tree Of Life

Draw yourself as a tree of life and then reflect using your journal and tapping on how deep you want your roots to grow, how flexible your trunk should be to withstand the storms of life, how far you want your branches to reach out, what kind of green dress you'd like to wear and what flowers, fruits or cones you would like to give birth to.

What does the completed picture look like? Is there something missing? What's surrounding the tree (grass, flowers, bushes, clouds, sun)? Are some parts bigger, more detailed, or more colorful than others?

How do you feel about the tree as a whole? Tap on what's coming to mind. If you like to add something after the tapping, just do it. Let your tree grow more and more beautiful and whole. Don't worry or overthink the process! Trust your subconscious and your emotional intelligence to understand and guide you on your healing journey.

The Tree Analogy/Metaphor

"The creation of a thousand forests is in one acorn." ~ Ralph Waldo Emerson

"Life without love is like a tree without blossom and fruit." ~ Khalil Gibran

An old man was planting a tree. A young person passed by and asked, "What are you planting?" "A carob tree," the old man replied. "Silly fool", said the youth. "Don't you know that it takes 70 years for a carob tree to bear fruit? "That's okay," said the old man." Just as others planted for me, I plant for future generations."

What does your tree look like? Do you have all of the following parts in your picture? What's missing? Just reflect without judgment.

The Ground/Soil
Where do you come from? Country, Mentality, Collective Consciousness, Religion, etc. The present landscape of action?

The Seeds – *SOUL & Birth – Heart Chakra*

Our soul? Innocent and free! Holding our gifts of creativity! Are you connected to your soul, your true authentic being?

The Roots – *Subconscious – Root Chakra*

Who is your family? Parents, Relatives, Ancestry? Do you feel safe, nurtured, and loved? Are your basic needs fulfilled? Are you resilient? Do you have good survival skills?

The Trunk – *Physical – Solar Plexus*

Reflect on your personality or sense of self: Who are you? What's your Identity? (The beliefs you have about yourself) What are your traits, skills, and values? Can you commit (to) yourself? Can you set healthy boundaries to protect yourself? Can you stand up for your convictions and persevere?

The Branches – *Emotional – Throat Chakra*

What is your path/purpose? What makes your life meaningful? What are your hopes, dreams, and visions? How do you express yourself? Do you allow creativity in your life? How do you express yourself?

The Leaves – *Mental – Sacral Chakra*

Relationships: Who do you allow to be with you in your life? Some people will stay life-long like evergreens. Some people only stay for a season and it's healthier to shake them off. Who did you lose due to big storms/catastrophes (all losses including death)?

The Fruits – Spiritual – Third-Eye Chakra

Do you allow yourself to be guided by Intuition? What legacies have been passed on to you? Who or what had a huge impact on you and your life? What are you grateful for? What did you learn/harvest? How did you grow personally?

_____

The Flowers & Seeds – SOUL & Infinity – Crown Chakra

What legacies would you wish to leave to others? What difference did you make in the world?

_____

Your personal TREE drawing

EFT Tapping Example after drawing your tree:

SOH: Even though I might not have been nourished and protected enough as a sapling and feel insecure lacking self-esteem, I deeply and completely love, accept and forgive myself.

Or

SOH: Even though I might have been overprotected and couldn't develop my own strength to protect myself from being used and abused, I deeply and completely love, accept and forgive myself.

Or

SOH: Even though I might not have been protected and my roots couldn't grow deep enough or were damaged by draughts and predators, I deeply and completely love, accept and forgive myself.

IE: I let my roots grow deep down into the soil to find nutrients and water necessary to sustain my life.

OE: I feel my sap running up and down freely, providing me with all the necessary nutrients.

UE: I allow my roots to entwine with other tree roots making a stable tree community in the forest.

N&C: My trunk stands firm, supporting my branches and carrying nutrients from my roots.

C&N: My trunk has enough flexibility to survive even the heaviest storms without breaking or being knocked over.

CB: I'm grateful for the layer of wisdom that is added to my rings of growth each year from my own life experiences.

H&H: I'm aware of my places of weakness and attend to them so I become strong and not be swayed by the winds of other people's opinions.

H&H: I'm confident in my decision-making abilities with the help of my inner guidance, listening to my intuition, following my heart and gut feeling.

UA: My branches grow upwards and outwards, they provide shelter from storms and shade from the sun.

LP: My branches bear fruit providing food and beauty for the eye of the beholder.

3rdE: My leaves turn to be colorful and bright, and I let them go with delight to see them sing and dance in the breeze and provide a mulch when they break down and once again enter the soil as my nutrients for times of need.

Thymus: I accept it as part of life that there are seasons to bear fruit and seasons where there is little or no fruit.

HHP: Whenever I go through transitions, I am like a tree that needs to rest, to conserve and renew its energy. I need to let go and celebrate change as the end of a season in my life. Sometimes I may even be transplanted if I move to a new location. I allow my roots the time to settle down, regrow maybe deeper than before, and find their food and nutrients. I love myself and accept that I will be vulnerable before I become stable again. These are the times I need to take the most care of myself for my roots to survive, thrive, and bear fruit in the next season.

Instead of HHP, you can start tapping around your eyes or on any other tapping point of your choice.

You can also use eye patterns and move your eyes in an infinity eight.
As before, I encourage you to trust your intuition. Don't just follow my suggestions.
Place your hands in a heart-healing position and take six deep breaths.
Reflect on how you feel. (You may want to jot it down in your journal)

Personal Achievement and Success

Draw an experience where you did something you didn't think you could do.
We all have accomplished something we didn't even dare to imagine.

Accomplishments show three things:

1. The precise actions you took in a given situation
2. The skills and abilities you used when facing a challenge
3. The results that you achieved

As you seek to identify your accomplishments, ask yourself the following questions:

- Have I received awards, special recognition, or a promotion?
- Have I developed a new system or procedure?
- Have I identified and resolved a problem to move forward faster?

- Have I been involved in a project that produced a specific result?
- Have I helped others achieve their goals through my leadership?
- Have I helped improve communications or relations?

Draw a symbol for ACHIEVEMENT, SUCCESS, REACHING A GOAL, etc.

Draw yourself as a superhero.

Step into the posture of a superhero and move like them.

Write a story about a superhero. It could have a title like "How… helped to…" or "How… saved the world…" etc.

Narrative therapy encourages clients to be their own narrators. **The goal is to empower them to feel in control of their own lives** by giving them control of the stories they tell. Narrative therapy separates the client from their problems and allows them to look beyond their own ego and pride. That's when the healing can begin. Separating a person from their problem encourages them to rely on their own skills to overcome even the biggest hurdles that exist in their lives.

DANCE AND/OR MOVEMENT THERAPY

helps individuals achieve emotional, cognitive, physical, and social integration. Beneficial for both physical and mental health, dance/movement therapy can be used for stress reduction, disease prevention, and mood management. In addition, the physical component offers increased muscular strength, coordination, mobility, and decreased muscular tension. Dance/movement therapy can be used with all populations and with individuals, couples, families, or groups. In general, dance therapy promotes self-awareness, self-esteem, and a safe space for the expression of feelings.

Freestyle dancing helps people get out of their heads and reconnect with their hearts, intuition, community, and inner wisdom. It is about moving authentically, gaining self-awareness, and allowing emotions to surface and naturally leave the body. The goal is to feel grounded and at peace at the end of the session.

Emotional Release Dance

Think about an event or memory that caused you emotional disturbance. Write it down in your journal or on a piece of paper.

Tap on each of the core feelings coming up while thinking about the memory. Finally, tap on the side of your hand: "Even though all those emotions had been with me for quite a while, I deeply and completely love, accept and forgive myself." Tap on top of the head and heart points (switching hands and repeating the statement): "I choose to release them with the following dance."

With the goal of "Letting Go" in your mind, put on some music. Don't think about your movements. Trust your body's knowledge and let the music and its rhythm move you. You may close your eyes for a short while. Make your movements big, involving your whole body. Express your feelings with your arms, hands, legs, feet, and posture. If you are angry, stomp your feet on the floor or punch the air as in shadow boxing. If you are sad, let those tears roll down your cheeks and keep on dancing. If you feel anxious include empowering expansive poses (for example the winner pose) and reflect on how they make you feel.

After the dance, sit down and silently tap through the sequence again, ending with your six breathes in a heart-healing position.

Slow Dance of Awareness

Put on some meditative music and move through the room as slowly as you can and with awareness of sensations from muscles and joints, postural sway and stability, and any emotional feelings, that these movements bring up for you.

Reflect:

Do I have to slow down on my dance of life?

Have I found my very own pace and rhythm?

Are my movements flowing smoothly or rather disrupted and unbalanced?

Am I taking big or small steps?

How does it affect my movement when I open my arms?

How am I impacted by different movements of my arms and legs or my whole body?

Is there anything that stops one of my movements from unfolding?

Can I dance through SHAME and EMBARRASSMENT?

After the music stops, write down whatever comes up and tap on it. You may also draw a picture (Mandala) of your experience and tap on the picture.

Walking Meditation With Emotional Release

Go for a nature walk. Think about something that weighs you down and tap on it while walking (emotional release through movement). If you feel angry push some dirt or gravel with your feet or just stomp on the ground with your boots. You may also take stones and throw them into a river.

Acknowledging present feelings transforms their power and enables a permanent release.

Place your attention on the part of your body where you're holding the trauma, and with every exhalation of your breath, focus on letting it go.

For the next 10 breaths and the powerful movements that may accompany them, just feel the painful sensation leaving your body. It may also help to make an audible tone or to run until you are exhausted.

After your walk, you may experiment with writing down your story of release. You can describe how nature helped you to release your trapped emotions. Perhaps you looked at the raging river and felt your sorrows washed away or you saw the leaves falling from a tree and felt a deep relief.

You may also put beliefs you want to release on pieces of paper and then ritually burn them and offer the ashes to the winds.

Try to feel the emotion leaving your body as the smoke of the fire rises to the sky. (You can always hold your ESR points)

Now, close your eyes and drop down into the sacred place of your heart, the very center of love and compassion.

As you breathe deeply, allow your heart to open.

Visualize and feel suffused with the light of love and compassion.

Feel its healing power, accept it, own it!

Allow this light to penetrate your body, soul, and your entire being, and let it create a deep sense of peace and protection within and all around you.

Chakra Freestyle Dancing

1st Chakra /// Root Chakra – Red
Why: To feel more rooted and grounded, to feel safe, to experience your basis.
Music: Ethnic music with lots of drums and beats. Didgeridoo sounds, low tones.
Movement: Leg and feet movements, emphasizing contact with the floor, circling counterclockwise with slow, stomping steps set to the rhythm of drums or shakers. Move your lower body to feel the ground; you may want to push it away or caress it, stamp it or 'kiss' mother earth with your feet.

2nd Chakra /// Sacral Chakra – Orange
Why: To boost your sensuality, creativity, and emotions.
Music: Jazz, soul, and Latin: anything that makes your hips move.
Movement: Move your hips/pelvis (belly dancing) in rotating motions and rhythmical flow. Enjoy the external expression of the feminine part inside of you.

3rd Chakra /// Solar Plexus – Yellow
Why: This helps you work on your willpower, confidence, finding your identity, and transformation
Music: Pop and rock: empowering, motivating, epic, and cinematic music that symbolizes the warrior inside of you, your courage, self-identity, and pride.
Movement: This chakra is around your midriff. The movements that go with it come from the martial arts: punch, slap, kick and include the poses of superheroes

4th Chakra /// Heart – Green

Why: To feel love, gratitude, compassion, and peace.

Music: Melodious songs, love songs, and classical piano pieces, often in minor because that makes the feeling go to the heart.

Movement: Open your heart by opening your hands and arms in front of your chest, bring your palms together in a prayer position in front of your heart, or open them as if you'd like to embrace or hug the world.

5th Chakra /// Throat – Light Blue

Why: For more self-expression, to speak your mind, and to communicate clearly.

Music: Songs you can sing along to, literally to let your voice be heard. For example "We are the champions.", "I want to break free.", "I am who I am." or "I'm coming out."

Movement: Allow your whole body to vibrate to the music. Feel your breath flow through your body, tremble, shake everything loose, hum, make some roaring noise.

6th Chakra /// Third Eye – Indigo

Why: When you want to work on your intuition, wisdom, imagination, and concentration.

Music: Fusion world music, with various styles, languages, and melodies in one track.

Movement: Move your head, face, and neck slowly, dance with closed eyes.

7th Chakra /// Crown – Purple or White/Gold

Why: To experience unity and oneness with the world, animals, people, the universe, everything.

Music: Spiritual music, mantras, overtones, singing bowls, meditation music, healing songs.

Movement: Become aware of the sphere around your body – and how it infuses everything. Feel the energy go up and down your spine, feel how all your chakras are working together. Stretch in all directions, move your whole body as if in a trance, humming, going down on your knees, then on the ground, moving in a snake-like motion, or curling up and being still.

BONUS

TAPPING SCRIPTS

- Daily Self-Care And Forgiveness Procedure By Iyanla Vanzant
- EFT Tapping For Grief
- Quick Good Morning Gratitude EFT Tapping
- Tapping For Abundance

DAILY SELF-CARE FORGIVENESS PROCEDURE BY I. VANZANT

ROUND 1

IE: I feel guilty and ashamed about some of the things that I've thought, said, and done.

OE: And the way that I have hurt myself and other people.

UE: I feel so guilty about some things I have done and have not done.

N&C: I feel so ashamed about certain things I have said and done.

C&N: I feel embarrassed about things I have said and done or not said and not done.

CB/KP: Someplace inside of me, it feels as if I am not a very nice person or a good person.

UA: I feel as if I'm not even worth forgiving.

LP: I am learning how to forgive other people, but I can't seem to forgive myself.

H&H: I am carrying around so much unforgiveness.

H&H: I feel so bad about myself, so unforgiving.

ROUND 2

IE: What if I stop beating myself up?

OE: What if it's time to start letting go of the guilt, shame, and unforgiveness?

UE: What if I acknowledge that everything is a lesson and that I was just doing the best I could?

N&C: What if I let go of the feeling that I can't forgive myself?

C&N: What if making that small choice starts the forgiveness process?

CB: What if I forgive myself a little at a time so that I feel safe and comfortable?

UA: What if I release all feelings of guilt, shame, and blame?

LP: What if I permit myself to transform my unforgiveness and self-judgment into peace and freedom?

H&H: What if nothing happens?

H&H: What if something does happen, something like I forgive myself?

ROUND 3

IE: It feels as if I am ready to release all forms of unforgiveness toward myself.

OE: It feels like I am open to the possibility of forgiving myself totally and completely.

UE: It feels like I am already forgiven by everyone for everything.

N&C: This forgiveness is very powerful.

C&N: I am tapping into the power of forgiveness right now.

CB: I am much more open and much better now.

UA: I am open to forgiving myself for creating or choosing experiences that require self-forgiveness.

LP: I have learned my lessons and released the need to repeat them.

H&H: I allow my mind and heart to experience total and complete forgiveness of myself for everything.

H&H: I know that everything has happened for my highest and greatest good.

Thank you! Thank you! Thank you!

ROUND 4

Now it's your turn! Tap on each meridian point speaking out loud what you are grateful for!

I am grateful / thankful for my wonderful mind and body / health / partner / home / friends etc.

EFT TAPPING FOR GRIEF

"We never lose our loved ones. They accompany us; they don't disappear from our lives. We are merely in different rooms." — *Paulo Coelho, Aleph*

SET THE INTENTION TO HEAL and remember to drink enough water before, during, and after the tapping!

Tap on the side of your hand and say:

"I have the intention to release the sadness and grief from my heart."

When you think about your loss, what emotion do you feel? Where do you feel that emotion in your body?

"Even though I feel this sadness in my heart, I Accept that I am feeling this way." (Tap on all the energy points)

Rate the intensity of your emotion on a scale of 0-10 (SUDS Rating-Subjective Units of Distress) 10 meaning – highest intensity (I feel terrible) 0 meaning – no intensity (I feel happy)

While rubbing the sore spot on your chest or tapping the side of either hand, repeat the following EFT Phrases aloud:

Even though I feel as if there is no way out for me and I don't know where to turn to, I deeply and completely/profoundly love, accept and forgive myself

Even though I feel so angry that I was left alone with a void, impossible to fill, I deeply and completely/profoundly love, accept and forgive myself anyway

Even though I feel as if this pain in my heart will never subside and I don't know how I am ever going to be able to move forward again, I deeply and completely/profoundly love, accept and forgive myself anyway

Now tap through the EFT sequence using the following energy points: If possible, tap on both sides of the face and body. (Use the palm to tap on the head and heart energy points)

Top of Head and Heart: I feel this tremendous pain in my heart

Take 6 deep breaths. Say: "I'm ready to release all this pain from my heart, mind & body NOW!"

IE:	I was left all alone
OE:	I feel completely NUMB
UE:	My mind is paralyzed, and I cannot have a clear thought
N&C:	I'm very angry for being left alone
C&N:	I don't feel like doing anything
CB:	I don't feel like living at all
UA:	This pain is so deep and overwhelming
H&H:	I don't know how to go on like this
H&H:	This turmoil of emotions and thoughts drive me crazy

Take 6 deep breaths & say: "I choose to release all this pain from my heart, mind, and body!"

IE:	I cry and cry all day long
OE:	I don't even want to get up in the morning
UE:	I don't want to get out of my home
N&C:	I don't want to talk to anybody
C&N:	This pain in my heart is overwhelming me!
CB:	I can't take it anymore
UA:	I'm so tired and burnt out
H&H:	I'm scared about my future
H&H:	I'm scared of facing life all by myself

Take 6 deep breaths. Say: "I acknowledge all those thoughts and emotions. I have a right to feel the way I feel. Now it's time to release all this pain from my heart, mind, and body!"

How do you feel? Rate your level of distress on a scale from 0 to 10, perform several rounds of tapping to bring the intensity down to zero.

Now it's time to reframe and expand your thinking and to open up possibilities:

IE:	What if I could relax just a little bit?

OE:	What if I could engage in new activities?
UE:	Maybe I can talk to somebody
N&C:	Maybe there is somebody who experienced similar pain
C&N:	What if I could reach out for help, to express freely what I am going through
CB:	I allow myself the time I need to grief and heal
UA:	Maybe I can release some of the pain right NOW
LP:	What if I can begin to feel more energetic NOW
H&H:	What if I started doing some self-care every day (just going for a walk)
H&H:	What if I introduced a new daily ritual to my life… just being open to the possibility that I can start new

Take 6 deep breaths. Say: "I CAN & I CHOOSE to release all this pain from my heart, mind, and body!"

IE:	What if I could mend my broken heart slowly with every passing day
OE:	I am open to breaking free from this pain
UE:	I deserve feeling a little joy in my heart
N&C:	I allow myself to embrace life again
C&N:	I cherish the memories no one can steal from me
CB:	I think of all the good times we spent together and celebrate your life.
UA:	I am grateful for all the blessings I received because of you
H&H:	I treat myself as I would a good friend
H&H:	I am ready to adopt a new sense of identity!

Take 6 deep breaths and say: "I wholeheartedly release all this pain from my heart, mind, and body NOW!" Let everything go, you don't need to keep it anymore!

"Gratitude Process"

Start with the **BUTTERFLY HUG** Method from EMDR Therapy.

1. Cross your hands and place them on your chest so each middle finger rests right below the opposite collarbone. Fan your fingers, resting them on your chest and your thumbs will be pointed towards your chin.
2. Hands and fingers must be as vertical as possible so that the fingers point toward the neck and not toward the arms.
3. If you wish, you can interlock your thumbs to form the butterfly's body and the extension of your other fingers outward will form the Butterfly's wings.

4. Your eyes can be closed, or partially closed, looking toward the tip of your nose.

5. Next, you alternate tapping your hands, like the flapping wings of a butterfly, slowly and rhythmically (left, right, left, right, etc.) for at least 8 rounds. Don't forget your deep breathing while you're fluttering your butterfly wings.

6. Gently observe what is going through your mind and body such as thoughts, images, sounds, odors, feelings, and physical sensation without changing, pushing your thoughts away, or judging. You can pretend as though your observations are like clouds passing by.

IE:	I am grateful because I will always love you and recall the happy memories
OE:	I am grateful because I have wonderful friends that support me
UE:	I am grateful because I know that my heart is healing
N&C:	I am grateful for the new beginnings that slowly will replace my pain
H&H:	I am grateful because I count the blessings I had throughout my life
H&H:	I am grateful because I know that I can give you a new place in my heart

"Gratitude bridges the past, present, and future; it allows us to retrieve the positive from the past and connects us with the present, and we embrace our good fortune." - Kingsley Gallup

QUICK GOOD MORNING GRATITUDE TAPPING

SOH: I deeply and completely love, accept and forgive myself!

I'm grateful for everything in my life that has led me to this moment as it has all been part of my unique destiny.

IE: I am grateful for who I am at a soul level.

OE: I am grateful for all my experiences because they provide valuable lessons.

UE: I am grateful for all life challenges because they provide opportunities to grow

N&C: I am grateful for my family & friends and their unconditional love & support

C&N: I am grateful for my ancestors living on through my blood

CB: I am grateful for all my pets and their daily gifts of unconditional love

UA: I am grateful for the beauty of nature that indulges my senses every day

LP: I am grateful for the possibility to choose a positive attitude that set me free

3rdE: I am grateful for the abundance I already have in my life and more to come

H&H: I am grateful for the ability to heal my body.

H&H: I am grateful for all the people who I have met on my journey for they have all been my mirrors and my teachers.

HHP.:   Thank you, thank you, thank you! Peace begins with me! Namaste!

EFT Tapping Script For Releasing Money Blocks & Inviting Abundance

Side Of Hand: "Even though I might not know how exactly this is going to happen, I intend to release all my resistance around money, and I deeply and completely love and accept myself for who I am."

"Even though I might not even know all my blocks buried deep in my subconscious, I intend to come into harmony with the energy of money, and I deeply and completely love and accept myself for who I am."

"Even though I might not know how I'm going to do it, I intend to come into alignment with my financial abundance and I forgive myself all the self-criticism and putting myself down."

First Round:

IE:	I allow myself to release all the resistance around money
OE:	I allow myself to let go of all my subconscious money blocks
UE:	I allow myself to be in harmony with money energy
N&C:	I allow myself to come into alignment with financial abundance
C&N:	I allow myself to receive financial abundance through known and unknown sources
H&H:	I allow myself to easily tap into financial abundance and attract it like a magnet
H&H:	I allow my heart and soul to come into alignment with the money

Put your hands in Heart Healing position and take six deep breaths

Second Round:

IE:	I truly love releasing resistance
OE:	I deeply enjoy letting go of my money blocks
UE:	I love feeling good about having money
N&C:	I love being in harmony with and attracting lots of money
C&N:	I love being in alignment with financial abundance
H&H:	I love manifesting money and abundance with ease
H&H:	I'm grateful for all the money I already have and will have

Put your hands in Heart Healing position and take six deep breaths

Third Round:

IE: I now choose to experience money as a spiritual resource in my life

OE: I know, there is enough money for everyone, and it is everyone's birthright to create wealth.

UE: I choose to create wealth right now.

N&C: I am ready to learn new ways of doing business and become a successful entrepreneur.

N&C: I am wise in my purchases and a good steward of my money

3rdE: Money is a spiritual resource to bless my life and help others in an honest and generous way

CB: I allow that money is flowing to me from known and unknown sources

H&H: I choose to rewrite the money story in my head and follow my spiritual guidance

H&H: My parents did their best, but I'm free to create more than what they chose to experience.

Put your hands in Heart Healing position, take six deep breaths and say the Ho'oponopono Prayer.

SOME ENCOURAGING QUOTES

"Healing takes time and asking for help is a courageous step." ~Mariska Hargitay

"Ask for help, not because you're weak, but because you want to remain strong." ~Les Brown

"Don't be afraid to ask questions. Don't be afraid to ask for help when you need it. I do that every day. Asking for help isn't a sign of weakness, it's a sign of strength. It shows you have the courage to admit when you don't know something, and then allows you to learn something new." ~Barack Obama

"Asking for help does not mean that we are weak or incompetent. It usually indicates an advanced level of honesty and intelligence." ~Anne Wilson Schaef, author.

"A little boy was having difficulty lifting a heavy stone.

His father came along just then.

Noting the boy's failure, he asked, "Are you using all your strength?"

"Yes, I am," the little boy said impatiently.

"No, you are not," the father answered.

"I am right here just waiting, and you haven't asked me to help you." ~Anon

REFERENCES

- Gary Craig www.emofree.com
- Roger Callahan www.tfttapping.com/ and http://rogercallahan.com
- The Kinesiology Institute https://kinesiologyinstitute.com/
- Expressive Art Therapy www.goodtherapy.org/learn-about-therapy/
- Dance Therapy www.adta.org/
- Freestyle Dancing www.dancedivine.ca
- Non-dominant hand drawing www.umamara.blogspot.ca/2015/09/controlled-remoteviewing farsight.html
- Ideograms www.federaljack.com/ebooks/Spirituality/ RV Manual.pdf
- Pain Management www.selfhypnosis.com/using-nlp-to-reduce-pain/
- Surrogate Tapping www.emofree.com/eft-tutorial/tapping-bonus/surrogate
- Proxy Tapping - Dr. Mercola www.healthypets.mercola.com/sites/healthypets/
- Sway Test www.tapintoheaven.com/2stuff/stufstest.shtml
- Self Muscle Testing www.amybscher.com/self-muscle-testing-the-sway-testor-
- idiometer-response/
- Emotions as Objects www.abh-abnlp.com/trance/scripts51.html
- Andrew Bryant www.selfleadership.com/metaphors-stories-and-nlp/
- Use of Metaphors in Counseling www.narrativeinstitute.org
- Metaphor Therapy www.goodtherapy.org/learn-about-therapy/
- Dr. C. Malchiodi "Think Metaphor" www.psychologytoday.com/blog/arts-and-health
- Nick Ortner www.thetappingsolution.com
- Iyanla Vanzant – Forgiveness EFT www.hhemarketing.com/author/vanzant/web/
- Dr. Bruce Lipton www.brucelipton.com
- Gwenn Bonnell www.tapintoheaven.com
- Dance/Movement Therapy www.goodtherapy.org/learn-about-therapy/
- History of Tapping www.goe.ac/history of tapping.htm
- Susan Shanley www.energymed.org/hbank/handouts/meridian tracing affirmations.htm
- 5 Elements www.wongu.edu.com
- Dr. Bridgett Ross www.rosspsychology.com/blog/cognitive-therapy-101-core-beliefs
- 5 Elements www.acupuncture-online.com
- 5 Elements www.5element.com.au/
- NLP Pain Management www.pradeepaggarwal.com/hypnosis-nlp.html

- Ho'oponopono www.hooponopono.org
- Ho'oponopono Thakurdas www.irp-cdn.multiscreensite.com/
- Chakra Teachings www.myss.com/chakras/
- Chakra Spinning Directions www.naturalchakrahealing.com
- Chakra polarities www.tantranectar.com
- Chakras www.myss.com/chakras/
- Chakra affirmations www.goodnet.org/articles/affirmations-for-each-chakar
- Chakra dancing www.happinez.com
- Bach Flowers bethterrence.com/bach-flower-wisdom-larch-remedy-of-confidence
- Sedona Method www.letmereach.files.wordpress.com/the-sedona-method.pdf
- Body Mapping www.new-synapse.com
- Body Map Story Telling www.migrationhealth.ca
- Eden Energy Medicine www.edenmethod.com
- Finger Holds www.flowsforlife.com

SHORT BIO

Monika Marguerite Lux is the founder of the BalanCHIng® Method which she developed over many years. She also developed "HeARTful Transformation Therapy", "The ART OF TAPPING" and "Emo-Flow Release Readings".

In her YouTube videos, Monika offers self-care tips, mindfulness exercises, guided meditations, and more.

As a therapist and healer, she is best known for her innate ability to intuitively identify the root cause of the unique patterns, beliefs, and negative self-talk that keeps individuals stuck. Over the past decade, countless individuals have experienced deeply transformative and long-term shifts from her integrative formula of intuitive counseling combined with Expressive Art Therapy, Systemic (Family) Constellation, NLP, and EFT Meridian Tapping.

Monika's passion for energy healing grew out of her own path of healing, and her desire to awaken to what is most vital and essential within herself. She is passionate about the transformational process and supporting others in opening to the truth and beauty that can come from the exploration of self. Holding each client's healing journey as unique, she helps them tap into their innate wisdom as a source for healing and personal transformation.

She helps people of all ages (teenagers, adolescents, adults, couples, and families) who are suffering from trauma, grief, and anxiety.

Her educational background includes a German Master's Degree in Applied Psychology, Applied Kinesiology and NLP Coaching, a diploma as a Relaxation Therapist focused on Qigong, and numerous energy healing certificates like Usui Reiki Master, Aromatherapy, Sound Healing, Matrix Energetics & Reconnection.

In addition to her private practice, Monika is a YouTuber, blogger, speaker, and workshop facilitator. As a professional photographer, her most favored non-traditional way of practicing meditation is to embark on a photo-taking spree with her Cocker Spaniel Luigi at breath-taking natural locations on Vancouver Island where she resides right now.

www.balanching.org   **www.youtube.com/c/balanching**

Printed in the United States
by Baker & Taylor Publisher Services